# reflecting pool

## POETS
### AND THE
## CREATIVE
## PROCESS

EDITED BY LAURENCE CARR

CODHILL
PRESS

2018

Codhill books are published by David Appelbaum for Codhill Press

**New York State Anthology Project**
**Reflecting Pool: Poets and the Creative Process**

Book Design by Jana Potashnik
BAIRDesign, Inc. · bairdesign.com

Cover art by Anne Gorrick

ISBN 1-930337-98-1

Printed in the United States of America

# CONTENTS

## ESSAYS AND POEMS BY HUDSON VALLEY POETS, MENTORS, WORKSHOP LEADERS AND EDITORS

DAVID APPELBAUM
FOUNDER, CODHILL PRESS

## FOREWORD

I was struck in my twenties by antiquity's conception of what poets are for. This was part of a larger identity crisis. I'd read Charles Olsen and from him derived the idea of a collective voice that would name the place—the mid-Hudson Valley—through a chorus of individual voices. It would articulate the topos through the particulars of history and presence, and verify how the local is the universal. This undertaking became Codhill Press's poetic mission, in its original formulation. The years, twenty of them, have brought an exemplification of that voice, voices really. Probably close to two hundred, if the several anthologies of regional poets were tallied. Plus single author editions of a couple dozen local poets. Somehow the totality of resonance enunciates what work of poetry obligates us here and now.

Of course, Codhill is more: spirituality, art, philosophy, story. They represent some other branches that grew from the vital poetic trunk of the tree. But the essence of its vision, the essence of its language, lies in the creative process of the poem. So we celebrate this new voicing with a hearty 'Bravo!' to all contributors. With more to come . . .

*...a collective voice that would name the place— the mid-Hudson Valley— through a chorus of individual voices.*

DAVID APPELBAUM

# SEASIDE

For every life, its vacant house,
a room whose ceiling is a hollow vat
a chair squats beside the pine nightstand
antediluvian scent of pitch.

The place must be there still
a cell that preserves life in
a womb that keeps from despair.

There, there was no desire
to unroll the bedding under the stars.

An owl or the kestrel
toward the edge of the grounds, by the sea
a wisp of curtain billows in night air.

A young girl sleeps on the cot.
She is over forty now.

In the stillness, nothing changes.
A candle on the table is burned down
but the room is not dark. It would always be so.
Apples kept in a bowl, a pitcher of water,
an unopened letter.

Below, a rock beach
reminded by softly lapping waves.
Far off, heat lightning flashes.
Outside, a dog would whimper.

# AN INTRODUCTION
## BY LAURENCE CARR, EDITOR

EVER SINCE I STARTED AS AN EDITOR with Codhill Press in 2007, I've wanted to create a "symposium" book, an anthology by and for poets. In between that beginning and now, I've edited or co-edited three other anthologies: *Riverine, an Anthology of Hudson Valley Writers; WaterWrites: A Hudson River Anthology; and A Slant of Light: Contemporary Women Writers of the Hudson Valley.* I've had the pleasure and honor of working with and helping to publish over two-hundred Hudson Valley poets and writers of fiction, memoir, and essays.

With *Reflecting Pool* comes something new for our readers: a book that features the poetry and essays of a group of established poets who also teach the writing of poetry on the college level, mentor poetry workshops and readings, and edit and publish the poems of others. This volume has truly become a symposium, a conversation among poets who share ideas about their creative process and how they nurture other poets with whom they work.

I have met and read with many of the poets here. Many are colleagues and friends. Some are poets I reached out to, never having met, but I had a feeling that they might be interested in this project. And it has culminated in a book where two dozen New York State poets (some not Hudson Valley residents) come together to share their creative ideas, exercises, and of course, poems.

I want to thank David Appelbaum, the founder and long-time publisher of Codhill Press for nurturing me as an editor and poet; Susannah Appelbaum, the current Codhill publisher, and my colleagues at SUNY New Paltz, who nurtured me as a mentor of poets and writers.

We, at Codhill Press, hope that the book will inspire poets, established and new, to continue their journey through this compelling and eloquent art form.

# DARING THE RIDICULOUS

EGO IS PROBABLY THE SINGLE BIGGEST HINDRANCE TO CREATIVITY in any field. Ego cajoles, "You are too good a writer to write a bad poem! Play it safe. Write what you know you can write, and be satisfied with that." True, ego keeps poets from embarrassing themselves with weak lines or failed ideas, but ego also discourages exploration and play, limiting the poem's energy and scope. Ego is the inner critic, second-guessing or outright ridiculing the poem-in-process that threatens to veer into wild vitality.

*Vitality arises from moments when the poem surprised the poet...*

Vitality is the quality that I most value in poetry. I want the poem to employ imagery and sound and thought and heart, but I need the poem to display the frisson of risk-taking. I want it to court the ridiculous. My favorite reaction to a poem is "Can the poet get away with this?" The "this" is vitality, which may take the form of an unexpected association or image, or a sudden shift of tone or focus. It may take the form of a lingering, or of a hastening onward. It may be repetition, and it may be elision. It may be daring a subject that is hackneyed, or a subject that is ridiculously unpromising.

Vitality arises from moments when the poem surprised the poet, who had the humility and grace to eschew ego—that is, to follow the poem rather than lead it.

Robert Frost expressed the importance of vitality when he declared, "No surprise in the poet, no surprise in the reader."

But here's my most serious charge against ego: ego takes the fun out of writing. I rail against the idea that writers are supposed to labor when we write. I think we're supposed to play. Play is exploration. It generates energy if nothing else, and energy is no small thing. I would argue that we need every bit of our energy for the painstaking labor of loving our poem into its final, polished form.

I count this as one of my greatest gifts as a poet: I am not afraid of the ridiculous. The vast majority of my ridiculous lines and drafts never leave my notebook, but they serve an important purpose: they keep me loose, open to discovery. Often enough they germinate into actual poems—if I can bear to see myself write some ridiculous, ego-shriveling stuff.

So how does one free oneself of ego? The answer is that I do not know. Practice? Practice, I guess. I do know this: my first responsibility as a teacher of creative writing is to keep my students brave. The classroom must be a place where it is safe to fail at writing a poem. Risk-taking— whether experimentation with new subject or form, or pushing subject and form to

>

> new places—enables poems to happen.
It enables poets to develop in skill and
scope. Risk-taking includes claiming
an obsession and burrowing into it ever
deeper. It means daring to be ridiculous.

## A FAVORITE EXECISE:
## "WRITE A BAD POEM"

This is one of the most successful
writing assignments that I present to
students, both undergraduate and MFA. In
order for this to work, the student needs
some understanding of what constitutes a
good poem, so I generally do not present
this exercise to undergraduates until later
in their semester. I find that MFA students
generally have read quite widely and hold
themselves to exceedingly high standards,
which makes them ideal candidates for
this. . . .

This exercise is designed to silence the
voice of the inner critic, and thus lead to
rich discovery. Here's how I present it:

No one in the world—including me—
need ever see this poem you are about to
write. This may be a poem you have tried
repeatedly to write. This may be a poem
you have never dared to write. It may be
a mere phrase or image that is stuck in
your head, or a memory that seems utterly
inconsequential.

*Give
yourself
permission
to describe,
ramble,
explore,
repeat.*

# Welcome the cliché, the confusing, the boring, the silly.

There is only one rule: write a bad poem. Jump into it. Welcome the bad lines as well as the good. Welcome the cliché, the confusing, the boring, the silly. The physical act of writing is what matters most. Feel the freedom and (even) joy of putting words onto the paper or computer screen. Give yourself permission to describe, ramble, explore, repeat. Do not worry about line-breaks or stanzas or spelling or momentary pauses between words. There is no way to fail this exercise except by not daring to do it.

Here's what happens, astoundingly often: after anywhere from five to ten minutes, the poet makes a discovery— an image, phrase, sound, memory, association, story—and bears down upon it. The writer discovers focus, engagement, depth. As if magically, this exploratory exercise begins to become an actual poem. Why? Because the poet has gotten free of the ego. The poet has gotten out of their own way.

Next, of course, the hard work of refining the poem begins.

## POSTCARD FROM THE ART COLONY

Small, to someone

Consider this: that anything can become a poem
if arranged into lines, anything, as long
as there is, behind the lines, a confidence, a willingness
to reconsider. People who work at Yaddo, I mean who live in town,
soon after dawn drive up the long hill. They walk through the mansion
carrying baskets of bed sheets. A young woman sits cross-legged
at the top of the Grand Staircase, polishing each spindle
with a spray-bottle of bright blue fluid, a small cloth.    ASSONANCE
This morning, outside my study window, a project:
the long-needle pine needs pruning. When I go to my desk,
I discover a ladder propped against the tree,
but no one in sight, as if this is all that is necessary:
choosing the tree, and the ladder,
and leaning them against each other.

SUZANNE CLEARY

# SAUSAGE CANDLE

*[A] long-time Manhattan resident . . .*
*Ms. [Fran] Lee advised radio*
*and television audiences on household*
*and consumer issues from the late 1940s*
*until well into the '90s. Her purview*
*ranged from cyclamates to asbestos*
*to how to make a candle from a sausage*
.

New York Times obituary, February 19, 2010

S

t

i

c

k

a wick in a sausage
and light it, and you've got
a candle, its flame fed by fat,
not that you'd burn it
on your birthday cake,
not that you'd light two
and process to an altar,
not that you'd want one,
even a small one, flickering
over your romantic dinner.
But the sausage candle gives light.
The sausage candle gives light.
Think of the books you could read
by the light of that candle,
think of the dark passages it might,
given the chance, illuminate.
It is better to light one sausage
than to curse the darkness.
Imagine, for a moment, you dare
set a sausage candle
atop your cake, and
you close your eyes and you wish.
Think of the wishes you could make
if you weren't afraid of the ridiculous.

THE FIRST BOOK OF POETRY THAT EVER INTRIGUED ME was Richard Brautigan's *The Pill versus the Springhill Mine Disaster.* I clipped it from my hometown's public library. My shabby adolescent Brautigan imitations were soon abandoned.

Later, during college, I rented a room in a tiny carriage house across the street from The Dickinson Homestead and took shortcuts through the Amherst village cemetery, passing Emily's grave on my way to classes at the University of Massachusetts. An influential course was American Romanticism, taught by Cynthia Griffin Wolff, who was writing a Dickinson biography. At the time, *The Norton Anthology of Modern Poetry* began with Walt Whitman (followed by Dickinson) and ended with another of my professors, then thirty-year-old poet James Tate. Under his guidance, I started writing verse. During those years, Donald Justice and Louise Glück came to campus to deliver poetry readings, leaving me awestruck. In town, the title of Charles Simic's *Return to a Place Lit by a Glass of Milk* seemed to sanctify Logos Books and could have served as the store motto. Like would-be snatches in a game of jacks, my philosophy about poetic craft, its range and possibilities, bob in these foundational memories. Ditto for scooped-up impressions of mentorship and the literary-arts community.

*Analogous to an argument or a journey, a poem also benefits from satisfying closure, whether arriving at epiphany or apocalypse.*

An apprenticeship in literary craft begins with studying wide-ranging traditions, genres, and schools, and fashioning self-discovery through one's own commitment to practice and experimentation. As Stephen King sums up in *On Writing: A Memoir of the Craft*: "If you want to be a writer, you must do two things above all others: read a lot and write a lot. There's no way around these two things that I'm aware of, no shortcut." Understanding fundamentals of writing holds equal importance. In the case of poetry, to my mind, this means recognizing and manipulating its essential components: linguistic compression, lyricism, economy of form, and centrality of the image. Analogous to an argument or a journey, a poem also benefits from satisfying closure, whether arriving at epiphany or apocalypse. To me, a successful poem achieves what critic Paul Fussell, in *Poetic Meter and Poetic Form*, calls "absolute density," meaning a coherence of parts—imagery, sound, tone, rhetorical devices, and themes. More simply, a good poem is one that calls audiences back for repeated engagement.

As teacher-mentor, I assign readings that represent a broad range of poetic styles and cultural outlooks, springboards to numerous writing exercises that introduce a variety of verse forms.

>

> These assignments intend to cultivate in beginning writers strategies that summon generative powers of inspiration combined with tools for revision. Overall, my emphasis is to encourage each writer to find a distinct "poetic identity" relative to language and subject matter. My own artistic arrows aim for small, tightly controlled poems, with images that target the depths of human intimacy and loss, reconciled against the vastness of the ocean and infinity of the cosmos—topics derived from personal geography, both literal and of the imagination. Consequently, common prompts to student writers include: Where and how is your life lived? Are your impulses urban or pastoral? What do you wish to communicate?

A good place to investigate that final question is in a writing workshop, what I prefer to call "peer review," designed to allow the group to collectively appreciate and analyze poems by others, offering constructive feedback. Whether formal (as in a classroom setting) or informal (organized among friends), a productive peer review instills in writers the attitude that composing for broad readership requires constant attention and vigilance. Indeed, following my observation that his sparse, elegant poems appeared divinely

*My own artistic arrows aim for small, tightly controlled poems, with images that target the depths of human intimacy . . .*

made, Simic told me (during an interview for *Chronogram* magazine), "There's no muse. I don't take dictation. It's really a slow process of making the poem—of endless tinkering and revising to make it sound inspired." Meanwhile, peer review may offer initiation into a community of writers, imparting a sense of being part of a literary tradition, among the most rewarding aspects of writing, in my view. Essential to joining the chorus is supporting fellow poets and writers by attending their readings, buying their books, and listening to their stories. I encourage students to partake.

Flipping open *The Pill versus the Springhill Mine Disaster* a half-century after its release, I believe many of Brautigan's verses still hold. Looking back on my own output, in the rare instance when a poem of mine feels satisfying to me—and that satisfaction has endured over time—a sublime happiness surfaces. I used to knit a lot, making gifts for relatives and friends. When you finish a sweater, mittens, or a scarf, you can say, "Here is a gift, something lovely but also utilitarian." A well-made poem can serve a similar function, albeit a metaphysical one. A poem can elevate the spirits, touching what some call the soul.

## EXERCISE: 5X5X5

**1** Write a poem of five lines or less.

**2** Include the following five elements arranged in any order: a color, a place, an animal, an active verb (other than "walk" or "run"), and an element of time.

**3** Construct your rough draft in five minutes.

Once you have completed this exercise, try revising the draft into a fully realized poem. You may decide to include additional lines and imagery or stick to the basic five-line format.

## POETICS: THE IMAGE

Two famous poetry dictums, attributed to modernist poets (who were also undergraduate friends at the University of Pennsylvania) follow:

"The natural object is always the adequate symbol." —Ezra Pound

"No ideas, but in things." —William Carlos Williams

The gist of this wisdom is that poetry relies on concrete imagery. The goals of the 5x5x5 poem exercise are to focus your attention on creating concrete language and images and to assist you in quick drafting.

PAULINE UCHMANOWICZ

# ELEGY FOR A SHIRT

Remnant from games
of capture the flag,
softened by time
into second adolescence,
this hand-me-down's
longevity stares
out mirrors at
my middle age.

Former flannel
of my brother,
one day finally
relinquished
to a closet reliquary,
will hang beside
our deceased father's
checkered woolen,
daring me to try on its
mortality for size.

# MECHANICAL DRAWING

Once fixtures in the halls of high school,
unapproachable boys, slender like slide rules,
supplied with graphite pencils, T-squares,
compasses and protractors,
would file to classes to manufacture
perpendicular lines, plot semicircles
and measure oblique angles,
labors as enigmatic as miniature
blue-lined boxes scoring graph paper.

Degrees apart between auto shop
and trigonometry geeks
they frequently played slide
trombone—typically boys
who ended up sloppily
startled by the brazen beauty,
instigating flings
on forbidden quadrants of playground,
sharp and pointed like
a mechanical-drawing gadget,
her rigid spread-V legs
drafting a blueprint of the world.

# CREATING IN COMMUNITY

*"Caffè Lena is widely recognized as the oldest continuously operating folk music venue in the United States. This little Caffè with humble beginnings is both grand and simple. The Library of Congress calls Caffè Lena "An American treasure," and we have been recognized by The GRAMMY Foundation for our important contributions to the development of American music. Yet we are proud to stay true to Lena's founding vision of simplicity, kindness to strangers, and art above profit."*

—from the Caffè Lena website.

I SHOWED UP AT CAFFÈ LENA ONE SUMMER NIGHT IN 2003 for a one-off poetry open mic. I'd heard about it when the assistant manager, Ann Hodge, contacted my writing group looking for a host. A Skidmore student involved with the café had initiated the event, and then backed out. MJ King, a vivacious fiction writer in our critique circle had immediately volunteered. I climbed the narrow staircase with some trepidation; the café was suspiciously dark and quiet.

I had some history with Caffè Lena. I was in a weekly writing group, since disbanded, that met at the café to critique and encourage, led by Franklin Whitney. Occasionally we'd have a reading at the café, with a mighty audience of ourselves and a couple of friends, billing ourselves as The Poetry Dogs. My daughter and I volunteered in the kitchen so we could see shows for free and my oldest son was involved in Channel Z, the student theater group that used the café's black box theater.

Ann was at the café that night and willing to chat with me. I don't remember exactly what we said to each other, but being in love with the Caffè Lena stage, I was desperate to have a regular poetry event there. Supporting poetry is part the café's mission: Music, Theater, Poetry,

>

> and they did book poetry events, like the Poetry Dogs, but only occasionally. Ann agreed to another one-night event later in the summer and that I could put it together. If it went well, we could try it monthly for a few months.

I felt less than ideally suited for the job, but I put the word out to the network of poets in the wider area. I let them know we had a chance to share poetry on this legendary stage but that we needed to turn out in force on Wednesday, July 30, 2003. Franklin Whitney would be the featured poet and we'd have an open mic surrounding his reading. The response was enthusiastic. We had around 60 attend the first night with such a preshow buzz that Ann had already booked us for another 6 months.

Fourteen years later, on the first Wednesday of every month, at some point in the I night find myself standing in the back near the sound equipment with Joe Duel, the sound guy, looking out at this well-loved, lovingly rebuilt, steeped in history, art space filled with poets and poetry fans listening to one poet on stage. And every month after the features have read, and we've taken a break, when I need to get us back to the program, I stand at the mic and look out over a room full of people who can't stop talking to each

*You don't know who your poem will speak to; we send signals into space based on hope.*

other about poetry. They're out there telling someone they loved their poem and why; they're buying each other's books, finding out about other readings. Every time I am thrillingly grateful that I get to be a part of opening this stage to the newly published, the frequently published, teachers, students, drifters, rhymers, slammers, traveling salesmen, those who are grieving, healing, and making their way by writing poems.

You don't know who your poem will speak to; we send signals into space based on hope. Every month I see poems connecting, sometimes with the whole room, sometimes it's one person. It's a tremendous risk and leap of faith to put your work out there, but surrounding yourself with other writers who are making that same leap is essential. They'll help you keep jumping.

# THE HAIKU

The Haiku realized
several syllables later
that weather patterns had changed
that she was wearing a bikini
over goose pimpled skin

In a cold blast of starting over
she grabbed a run-on sentence
out of a five page essay
on the Industrial Revolution
wrapped it scarf-wise around her neck

She knitted a thick dress
out of lines unraveled
from random Wikipedia entries
The loop and bind of wooly facts
kept her free from artistic drafts

She plucked a hat
from the local section
of her daily newspaper
let minor assaults and drug busts
insulate her scalp

She fashioned boots that looked
exactly as if they were durable
from volumes in Wal-Mart's
book aisle, laced them tightly
to the soles of her mud stained feet

She started eating pizza
in front of the TV
No more baby salad greens
drifting gently onto her plate
She took to sleeping late
and avoiding mountains

She kept in touch with her sister
haikus, listened to their short
bursts on waterfalls and birds
but took no joy
in the conversations

She longed for work
that was fleshed out
something *how to or hilarious*
*something unputdownable or*
*authoritative and vast in scope*

She started watching sunsets while eating
ice cream and weighing her options. A cookbook
occurred to her during one fiery orange display
*A cookbook*, she considered, *is something*
*to drip batter on, leave open*

*to the heartbreak of unpredictable grease*
*A cookbook*, she thought, setting down
her bowl and licking her spoon
*with lazy, rambling directions*
*recipes with 17 ingredients each*

## WHAT IF

Emily Dickinson's rise
to poetic stardom was a reality
TV show? Think a Victorian house
with staid, heavily placed furniture
a white figure wisps across a distant
hallway, cut to a bee hovering
studiously over a patch of red clover

Characters will include an absolute
silence, a wind, sometimes soft
sometimes wailing, death, and
a rotating cast of flowers and insects

Emily herself stipulates
we can only film her in passing

Each confessional is a poem
ink spreading on paper
abandoned in random spots
discovered by the camera
lying amid, say, the debris
of a finished breakfast

*pleasure of unexpected*

*. . . nihilism isn't cynicism, but its opposite, an attempt to get to the truth of issues.*

I'M ALWAYS STRUCK BY HOW MY POEMS, NO MATTER THE CONTENT, SEEM TO SPEAK TO MY PSYCHOLOGY. I recently wrote one that I thought was merely a "writing manifesto," referencing Turgenev's novel, *Fathers and Sons*, and the concept that dominates that book, what is referred to in it as *nihilism*, defined by the protagonist son as the repudiation of his father's values. I claim in the poem that nihilism isn't cynicism, but its opposite, an attempt to get to the truth of issues. I thought of it as a defense of a critical stance I was adopting at the time in a lot of the poems I was writing—poems critical of our culture in general, its politics, its values. I thought of the poem as merely a poem of statement.

Now when I look at it, it's obvious to me it's not after *the truth* at all. I was merely repudiating the values of my own father, because it was those values, or the way they were conveyed to me, that had made me feel bad about myself most of my life. The poem may be a manifesto still, but more of a psychological one, a proclamation of my independence and self-worth, rather than a philosophical or aesthetic declaration. The poem is called "the most difficult thought," which is a reference to Nietzsche's descriptor of nihilism, which is apt for my reading of the poem. To repudiate the values of my father is, for

&gt;

> me, the most difficult thought, because of my love for him and my respect for what he valued and the life he led living out those values. But the interesting paradox in that process, which is precisely what makes it "most difficult" for me, is that I had to repudiate my father to love him. Without the repudiation, there could be no self by which to love. I'm not sure the poem is saying all *that*, but now I see that it enacts it.

I'm sure my love for writing is more complicated than that. Surely we can't reduce *everything* to our psychological idiosyncrasies. Why do I pay the utmost attention to form, for example? Why do I labor over finding the right word, and not just the right word for the meaning but the right *sounding* word? I suppose I could reduce even those impulses to the impulse to heal myself psychologically—that the poem is, say, enacting my psychology *by way* of pursuing a kind of aesthetic excellence—but I suspect what's really going on is more complicated. It's probably the case that the pleasure of writing comes from a confluence of several impulses: the psychological, yes, but also the aesthetic, the political, the ethical, the sexual even, and so on. The pleasure, in fact, of writing poems, and reading them, comes precisely from the poem's capacity to speak to multiple

*Without the repudiation, there could be no self by which to love.*

impulses at once. I also write academic and personal essays, and while they satisfy a certain impulse—the impulse principally I suppose for what we might call prefrontal lobe clarity—they don't ring the bell for me. Poems ring the bell.

What am I to do with this insight? Probably nothing, for the pleasure comes from the moment, emerges from the ground up, so to speak. For the same reason that writing poems satisfies me in a way that writing essays doesn't, I don't want to dwell too long on an abstract principle. I recently wrote a poem that likens a swarm of starlings to a blue whale rolling over in the sky. I don't know how that image speaks to my psychology, but I won't dwell on it. That blue whale—who probably represents me in the poem—is having too much fun.

# THE MOST DIFFICULT THOUGHT

nietzsche's phrase for the
claim that nothing has meaning
turgenev's *fathers*

*and sons* tells the tale
of the son instructing the
father that the most

useful thing he can
do is disavow his values
and refers to this

act as nihilism
the rejection of them all:
truth community

greed sincerity
goodness profit sin joy sloth
forgiveness envy

doubt mercy justice
love wrath and god all on the
scrapheap of human

culture this is not
for me cynicism but its
opposite: get so

deep in the mud you
can clearly see what's not at
the root of it all

CORY BROWN

# EXPERIENCE-DEPENDENT NEUROPLASTICITY

the phenomenon
neuroscientists observe
in which the brain as

they say "takes the shape
of what it rests on" . . . so if
i focus on those

experiences
that make me feel grateful to
be alive . . . the feel

of my feet in warm
sand the sight and sound of a
child reading aloud

as she scans each line
with her finger a hawk in
a bare winter's sky . . .

then i'm shaping my
brain to be less reactive
anxious and sad that's

good it means i can
control who i am but they
also say two-thirds

of the brain is as
set in its ways as a log
rotting in a swamp

## POETIC LICENSE: BREAKING RULES THE RIGHT WAY

TYPICALLY, I BEGIN ANY CLASS OR WORKSHOP IN POETRY BY ASKING PARTICIPANTS TO IDENTIFY FORMAL AND STYLISTIC HALLMARKS that differentiate poetry from prose. One difference that always receives mention is the license to defy many of the conventions governing expository prose. In poems, readers are apt to encounter linguistic oddities of many kinds, including non-standard syntax, punctuation, and word usage. As would-be poets, workshop participants welcome this liberation from linguistic conventions. At the same time, however, they acknowledge that departures from normative usage often constitute a source of puzzlement and, indeed, sometimes unwelcome difficulty when these occur in *other people's* poems. Discussion ensues: why do poets create run-on, incomplete, or otherwise malformed sentences? Why do they invent new meanings for existing words or coin new ones? Why would they risk confusing or alienating readers, except in the interest of achieving otherwise unobtainable effects? We look closely at varied examples of rule-breaking in writing by post-WW II poets, considering what is accomplished in each instance by a poet's defiance of prescriptions for ordinary correctness.

The last line of "The Mouth of the Hudson," by Robert Lowell, for instance,

*Why do they invent new meanings for existing words or coin new ones?*

offers an intriguing example of an apparently misplaced or misused word. After describing a scene marked by industrial waste and polluted air, the poet-speaker sums up his impressions: this is an "unforgivable landscape." Since only humans can require forgiveness, such anthropomorphic usage, applied to the urban New York—New Jersey region as a whole, appears awkward and undiscerning. The "landscape" has not ruined itself, after all, and stands in no need of forgiveness. It is the human inhabitants who are responsible for the filth that is poisoning river, ground, and air. Struck by the apparently wrongheaded placement of a crucial modifier, readers are invited to ponder the reasons for Lowell's chosen phrasing. He is reminding readers, perhaps, of the human tendency to shift blame: instead of castigating ourselves for the environmental destruction we have wrought, we vilify the ugly, reeking places we have created. The scene depicted in the poem provides vividly "unforgivable" evidence of a culpability we tend to deny. If Lowell had applied his term of moral judgment directly to humans, the effect would be preaching and obvious: his message would be easily dismissed by readers who have heard exhortations about environmental responsibility all too often. By displacing his modifier, forcing

> readers to ponder the reasons behind that
displacement and locate the real target of
his rebuke, Lowell hopes to inspire more
active acknowledgment of responsibility
for the "unforgivable" consequences of
human technological and commercial
ambitions.

Gwendolyn Brooks provides a
conspicuous instance of the license to
coin new words in her poem "'pygmies
are pygmies still.'" Contrasting two
clearly symbolic groups ("pygmies"
and "giants") throughout the poem,
Brooks sets up a series of contrasts. The
"giants" are associated with elite status:
long-standing privilege has rendered
them helpless and lazy, draining them
of any urge to achieve. They "bleat" and
"pound[] breast-bone punily," never
undertaking any demanding enterprises.
In contrast to the high-achieving pygmies,
who obtain marvelous views and "expand
in cold impossible air" at the tops of
mountains they have climbed, the giants
have "reached no Alps." In their own
eyes, the giants remain preeminent, but
their lack of effort and accomplishment
strips their self-image of authenticity: it
is a "poor glory" that they enjoy. The word
Brooks coins to describe their unearned
complacency is "giantshine." Severed
from the context created by the poem,

*. . . long-standing privilege has rendered them helpless and lazy, draining them of any urge to achieve.*

*the right to
break rules
must be
earned*

readers might interpret this conjunction of familiar words to mean something like *big glow.* The text of the poem pushes readers to the intended meaning effortlessly, however: "giantshine" represents the inflated sense of self-worth characterizing those the poem denotes as "giants." They make a big show out of nothing, thinking of themselves as radiant centers of the universe even as they "bleat and chafe in their small grass." The poet might have drawn on the existing term "blowhard" to describe them, but her newly invented term does a better job of conveying their wildly-overestimated sense of their own importance. This example is useful in demonstrating that poets must provide details enabling readers to interpret any new usages or coined words accurately. The introduction of invented terms must be justified in context: readers must be persuaded that existing vocabulary is insufficient to convey the desired significance and effect.

Drawing attention to nonstandard language use in successful poems, my goal is to show apprentice writers that the right to break rules must be earned: every apparent mistake in diction or construction must achieve an effect so intriguing or powerful that it comes to seem breathtakingly inevitable.

>

> Each disruption of convention must
be perceived by readers as the best or,
indeed, the only way to express what
is at stake at that moment in a given
poem. Close examination of the work
of accomplished poets usually serves
to extinguish the assumption, common
among inexperienced writers, that in
poetry all the rules are suspended all the
time. Instances of linguistic eccentricity
must reflect creative innovation—the
deliberate flouting of principles a writer
obviously has mastered—rather than
laziness or ineptitude. Having examined
the brilliant wrenching of compositional
norms by acknowledged masters,
aspiring poets grow embarrassed to
defend grammatical and syntactic faux
pas with the justification that in poetry
anything goes. If they leave the workshop
convinced that deviation from linguistic
conventions is acceptable only when it
serves discernible purpose—rather than
as a handy excuse for failure to wrestle
sufficiently with recalcitrant drafts—
then they have absorbed at least one
foundational principle of good poetry and
been disabused of a widespread myth.

*linguistic eccentricity must reflect creative innovation*

JUDITH SAUNDERS

# SUNSET: BEACON, NEW YORK

Streaks of vivid pink
arc above the valley, stream
across the deep-blue dome

of sky through smudged gray sprays
of cloud (all flashing gold)
curve around Mt. Beacon

down to the western riverbank,
enclosing in gaud
a landscape suddenly small,

inside the opal globe of evening
transfixing us
in this lapidary moment.

JUDITH SAUNDERS

# MILTON TURNPIKE AFTER RAIN

A luminous Wedgwood of chicory
and Queen Anne's lace, cheerfully
untidy, crowds the roadside,
admits a few decorous blossoms
of wild white morning glory,
foregrounds casual spurts
of purple (loosestrife and thistle
or mauve of milkweed) that lure
a passing swallowtail to feed:
August's finest flora
freshly watered and shined,
capping summer with a flourish.

## LISTENING AS PART OF THE CREATIVE PROCESS

*What is helpful is to listen to the writer, then give back what you remember, what stays with you. Each writer is finding his or her way to voice. It cannot be coerced, and it cannot be given form or shape by anyone else.*

—Pat Schneider

EVERY HUMAN BEING HAS A STORY TO TELL, real or imagined. My story, and yours, is one more addition to the ongoing saga of the human experience, what it feels like and means to be alive.

Wallkill Valley Writers (wVw) prepares a space that welcomes and encourages, inexperienced to published, writers to tell their stories through the written word. Writers are encouraged to play, explore, and discover the content and shape of their stories. The interaction between writers and creative listeners guides writers to what is strong and what stays with us.

As a workshop leader, I have developed a deep appreciation for the role of listening in the creative process. We practice listening as an active skill. Writers are directed to listen completely, rather than partially; to listen partially is to allow our minds to wander to a story of our own, or to begin to think of an oral response we might give a writer before hearing the complete draft read aloud in the group. We do not listen *for*, that is *for* what needs to be corrected, what is missing, what we might change. Listening *for* is reductive, not creative. We listen with the writer. Eudora Welty described listening as "an early form of participation in what goes on."

>

> As listeners, we are co-creators, along with the writer, in the process of locating vitality in a first draft. We listen, then respond to newly written, first draft work in workshop. We give back to the writer our experience of the draft: what moves us, where we feel power and strength in the words, where we flow with the music of the language, where the images create movies of the mind, where we learn something or feel something new, where we feel we could hug or smack a character, where we are surprised by the way words can rub together to make magic. We listen and learn from the responses given to each first draft, not just our own. Every writer improves their access to memory and imagination, as well as their craft.

In wVw workshops, we have listened to first draft writing that feels "physically as if the top[s] of [our heads] were taken off." (Emily Dickinson) We have listened to short stories, sections of novels, passages of memoir, and poems of emotional genius and striking craftsmanship. Much of this amazing work may never be public or heard outside the safe space of a wVw workshop.

As a community writing workshop and community of writers, wVw encourages and supports writers to make their work public. Making work public, publication,

*We listen and learn from the responses given to each first draft, not just our own.*

takes many forms: reading at open mics and local spoken word venues, self-publication for family and friends, self-publication with self-marketing, publication in local and national journals or anthologies, local or national literary contests, publication with regional or national book publishers, archived in local historical societies, or published online.

The options are too numerous to list. wVw writers have made their voices public in most of these venues. Currently, a writer has a contract for a trilogy of young adult novels, the first of which has been published. Still, there are writers whose only desire is to create and to do so well with integrity and craft. It is enough to "publish" their work in a select community of writers.

Wallkill Valley Writers is an affiliate of Amherst Writers and Artists and adheres to the AWA tenet that "Art belongs to the people. . . . Art is the creative expression of the human spirit, and it cannot. . . . be limited." Human beings are creative animals. wVw works with anyone who desires to claim writing as their art.

## AFTER THE FLOOD

May you remember where ya't
a second line isn't parallel
but a strut as wavy as the river's
crescent you call home.

May you remember—yeah, ya right
a street car named Desire was a play
on words rolling electric through
housing projects without any.

May you remember the low down nine
where shotguns were homes
and a clean shot from the front through
the back door saved lives.

May you remember red beans and rice
with hot sauce and don't never
put no tomatoes in your gumbo—
what do Carolina folks know about good food.

May you remember lagniappe
a li'l something extra
the weight of a generous hand added to
a pound of smoked sausage.

May you remember how she rambled
big and bawdy and loose
kept dark secrets behind carnival masques
burned her sins to ash on the altars of saints.

May you remember funerals are parties
after a closer walk with thee
turn your back on death's iron gate
strut your stuff, jazz it up.

And may you always remember
le bontemps roulez.

## THE SEMINAR

Iron shackles clanked
onto the table. Placed among
books and papers, rough metal
smothered musings, silenced

pens scratching for understanding.
Iron gave weight
to studied words about
whips and chains and runaways.

Bulk made light
pursuit of metaphor and simile.
Passed from hand to hand,
each left and right

a balance pan lifting
the shackles up and down
to gauge their heft. Fingers
rubbed the biting metal.

Touch taught
what words could not,
how the soul
wears raw.

A perpetual caravan
of red and ragged
flesh moves confined
through time and space:

shuffle aboard slave ships,
stumble in coffles sold deep south,
shamble in chain gangs along dusty roads,
step aboard downstate busses for upstate prisons.

# DIALOGIC POETRY

### 1.

WHEN I READ, PICTURES FORM IN MY MIND just as if I am remembering something that actually happened to me. Scenes—the one in the book, the ones in my memory—seem equally real and unreal. Both play in Technicolor. At times, however, the scene in the book is far more evocative, far more memorable, than the muted filmstrip of my life.

In these instances, the bright images of a story or essay—the characters' environments, their beautiful articulations—run alongside the film of where I was when I was reading: in the detached backseat of a Buick propped against the wall of a mechanic's garage. The novel may have been filled with emotion and with fine ideas while my own backdrop reeked of the tinny stink of motor oil, the fragrant sticky grit coating the tall shelves lined with spare parts, Snap-On tools, and headlights—the same grit that coated my stepfather, a mechanic, bent over an engine as a single bulb dangled from a tar-coated wire.

It's no wonder that I fell so hard for poetry. Poetry has traditionally insisted on Beauty (capital B) and much of it, even today, attempts to fulfill the broad, variable requirements of this tradition (at least some of the time). Poetry's

>

*The novel may have been filled with emotion and with fine ideas while my own backdrop reeked of the tinny stink of motor oil . . .*

> purpose has been debated over the ages—
must it deal with tragedy, with love, with
monumental events, with Nature, with
God's hand made visible? Should it evoke
fear or pity in readers? Should it comfort,
confess, amuse, goad? Yes, I say. All of
the above. Poetry must express something
blindly reached for, vaguely remembered,
a music that emerges from inchoate
longing. Its expression must remain
mysterious, contradictory, tragic, perhaps
bewildering. Only then can we find *beauty*.

My father's family lives near the
Cherokee Reservation in the Great
Smokey Mountains of North Carolina,
and my summers were spent in a world
of startling beauty—and tragedy. In the
Nantahala Forest are trees so enormous
two people holding hands can't circle
them; curling fiddlehead ferns,
magnificent waterfalls, and, nearly every
weekend, car crashes; nearly every month,
a murder. Nowadays, the opioid crisis has
made death commonplace in Appalachian
communities, but when I was a child,
before the casino opened, the seedy
downtown was notorious for its tourist
traps, its drunks, and its dangers. The
poems in my most recent book, *Cherokee
Road Kill*, are set in those mountains and
a woman I knew—sweet Louise—killed
by her lover, is the inspiration of its long
sequence of poems.

*. . . my summers were spent in a world of startling beauty— and tragedy.*

Louise worked at the local Christian bookstore specializing in self-help and inspirational texts: Tammy Faye Bakker's tell-all, Maria von Trapp's *Sound of Music*, Dale Evans's remembrance of an adopted daughter killed in a bus accident (God's will!). There were a few classics and Louise directed me, a lonely kid she recognized as a reader, to ones she thought I should read: Anne Frank's diary (my first exposure to the Holocaust); *The Turn of the Screw, The Sword in the Stone*, among others.

Many of the poems in this collection are from both Louise's perspective and from her murderer's, imagistic ticker tapes playing simultaneously.

> **2.**

As a teacher of poetry workshops,
I try to get students to key into these
filmstrips running through their minds.
I ask them to read aloud, to close read,
to memorize and recite—in other words,
to immerse themselves in poetry. I want
them to take risks, to write what's difficult
for them, to risk failure as they try on
new perspectives, new voices, and new
geographies.

My biggest concern is with homework.
How do I get students to really read a
poem—not just skim it? What assignments
will ask them to consider line breaks,
vocabulary, metaphor, message, puns,
so that our discussions are informed?
Barring that, what writing can I give them
at the beginning of class that gets them
started on the work of close reading and
stymies quick-takes?

To help my students come to a deeper
understanding of the poetry I assign, I ask
them to compose 3-4 questions at home
after reading a poem and come in with
these questions to our workshop meeting.
I then assign groups of 4 that work
together, discussing the questions until
each group comes to a consensus about the
phrasing and intent of one collaborative
question—Question A from Group A;

*I want
them to
take risks,
to write
what's
difficult
for them . . .*

*That a poem can assert one thing and, just as easily, assert its opposite, its negative number.*

Question B from Group B; etc. We put these questions on the board and discuss their bones (structure) and their meat (content), and then assign each question to different groups: Question A to Group C, Question B to Group D, etc.

The small groups write together to create a group-answer which we then share aloud and discuss. I've found this to be a wonderful way to get students to accept the possibility of multiple interpretations— of the possibilities of questions and the possibilities of answers—and that there's not just one "right" answer and many "wrong" ones. That a poem can assert one thing and, just as easily, assert its opposite, its negative number. That two filmstrips can run simultaneously, side by side, as we read—or write—a poem.

# KNOT OF LONGING

*We are made/ in a thin thread.*
—Cole Swenson

Long before he had just cause
he let himself long
for Out.
For the cardinal in & Out
of the yard
splash of blood
against the high wall
clouds describing the curve
of Out.
He recused himself
from petty quarrels
over contraband
precedence
mops and spatulas
and tasted
clots of eggs,
felt again
the crisp give
of a driver's seat.
On his bunk he
was the crosshatch
of this fifth
year of In, dreaming
scraggly ends of
branches
then under his sleep-soft
hands the chub trunk
of evergreen, turpen-
tang of needles.

# CHEROKEE ROAD KILL

*proper nouns
- ground us, put us in place
- specificity brings us in closer*

Every year, spring snow sugars the road and a lank-
haired son of Sequoyah High School
closes long lashed eyes in Cullowhee and opens them—?   *will he open them again*

Like Kenny Arrowhead who kissed me in the back of his   *2 passions*
brother's Corvette after his brother   *love + anger*
strangled his wife—that other kind of crash.   *car*

Kissing, we drank deep from a clay-sided well sweaty as your
upper lip, spicy as fern. Stars were lures in the
Smokies' cleft.   *dreams   catch you*

His brother on the run, scarfing
wrinkled juniper berries. Maybe vomiting pine.
Snapping bloodroot to sip red sap
or sucking a redbone cottonmouth
flat as a dollar bill, maybe.

He is my fist pulling
trillium, Virginia snake-root from the red clay
bank of Pisgah as Kenny Arrowhead, a
cash crop, skids the glistening washboard turn into the Nantahala
and
flips his Jeep Cherokee.

A throttled gasp and I am
trolling the pools of Pisgah,
silt-sinking and whiskery catfish god cruising
the dark cleft.

*What movements rill the surface of what he breathes?*

*desire + dangers*

LUCIA CHERCIU

## A PERSONAL ESSAY

I TEACH CREATIVE WRITING: POETRY and a wide range of writing courses at Dutchess Community College in Poughkeepsie, where I have been working for sixteen years. In my writing classes, my role is to encourage students to discover their passions, find poets and writers that they can connect to, develop their own unique style and voice, and explore the possibilities of writing in order to improve their own lives and strengthen their communities.

*I believe in a literature of inclusion*

I believe in a literature of inclusion, so every semester I require texts that bring light to my students' lives and motivate them to listen to different points of view and look at writing as a means of expression and bettering themselves. For example, last semester in my Creative Writing course I required the book *Counting Descent* by Clint Smith. We read the whole book for the class and students wrote a book review that they published on Amazon or tried to submit for publication to literary magazines. Students also listened to some of Clint Smith's TED talks about the importance of speaking up.

In my own case, as a reader, I find that I resonate with one poem out of fifty, and I believe it is my responsibility to help connect the right people to the right books. When someone says they do not

*As children, we all learned to savor the taste and sound of words, to play games and sing nursery rhymes.*

like poetry, it might mean they haven't yet found a poem or a writer to connect with. When I choose the readings for each course I include texts that mirror the diversity of my students so they can discover literature as a means of communication and of being in the world.

In addition to writing a book review, the student-writers in and I have developed a Service Learning Project where we visit an elementary school in the area and work with fifth-grade students. Service Learning has provided my students and me with a tremendous source of energy and enthusiasm. When we work together with ten-year-old children, we learn about their dreams and share their joy of playing with words, writing together, and discovering the music of language. Having fifteen college students in the same room with twenty fifth-grade students and writing poems together added a new dimension to the course. As children, we all learned to savor the taste and sound of words, to play games and sing nursery rhymes. Writing together with ten-year-old students reminds my class about the times when they discovered the delights of language.

I am well aware of these delights of language because I am bilingual, and every day I learn new words and keep lists of

> words that I love both in English and in
Romanian. I come from a culture where
children learn several foreign languages in
school, starting from kindergarten, and I
myself studied Latin, French and German.
Because I write both in English and in
Romanian, I encourage students to listen
to words the way they listen to music,
and to learn to appreciate the power and
pleasure of language. Writing poetry helps
students to discover the joy of language
that we all experienced as children or
witnessed when our children spoke their
first words. A Creative Writing course
helps students to discover a new world.

Writing in two languages has also taught
me that a style of writing that is favored
in one culture can be considered obsolete
in another, and every culture has its own
norms, expectations, and definitions
when it comes to writing, even at the level
of punctuation and sentence structure.
Being bilingual enriches one's view of
writing and allows a writer the respite to
look at the world from different points
of view. This is particularly meaningful
in writing poetry, where often words,
expressions, and accomplishments
in terms of craft and form cannot be
translated from one language into
another.

Moreover, in a society where everything
is about money and consumerism, poetry

*Being bilingual enriches one's view of writing and allows a writer the respite to look at the world from different points of view.*

# I encourage all of my students to attend the readings . . .

becomes a form of prayer in which the individual is free to express oneself, discover one's own place in the world, and reinvent oneself through language. Some of my students are working full-time jobs and raising a family while attending college full-time and paying for their own education. Their voices are often left out of the canon, and their point of view is ignored. That is why creating a space for reading and writing poetry offers them the opportunity to discover who they are and reinvent their position in the world in their own terms.

My role as a teacher is to introduce them to a wide variety of writers and writing styles so they can see that their possibilities are endless. Dutchess Community College organizes a reading series titled From Process to Text, and many poets in the area have been invited to read from their work. I encourage all of my students to attend the readings, and ask them to write a response to the work they have listened to. In this way, students learn that there are various styles of poetry, and they have to discover a style that speaks to them and represents their own interests and aspirations.

>

> ## A WRITING EXERCISE

Draw a vertical line in the middle of the page and create two columns. On the left side, write a list of words that you love, maybe for the way they sound, their connotations, or because your mother or someone else you love uses these words and they have a deep meaning for you, such as *dahlia, gratitude, respect, trust,* and *memory.*

In the right column, write a list of words that you dislike because of the way they sound or for no clear reason, such as *procrastinate, persnickety, cantankerous, whatever,* and *robust.*

Once you have a full page of words, choose five evocative words from each column and write a poem that includes them.

This exercise can be changed into a group or class project by choosing as a class five words from the ones that have been listed, words students agree on, and writing a poem including these five words. For example, you could write a poem using the words *liver, taxes, moist, payday,* and *home.*

# ONLY TWO MINUTES FROM OUR HOUSE

Some stories say Chicory refused
to give a glass of water to a thirsty old man
so she was turned into a flower.

Others say her fiancé died in the war
and she was left behind
to cry on the side of the road.

She was in love with a sailor
who didn't return,
so every day she waited for him.

One morning the Chicory fairy
was bathing in dew when the sun
saw her and fell in love.

He sent the morning star to propose
on his behalf, but she rejected him,
so the sun turned her into a flower.

Others say you can unlock a treasure trunk
with a thread of chicory,
blue petals cutting gold.

We drank it during Ceauşescu's time
in adulterated coffee, yet now
we find out it's good for us.

Its hypnotic flowers
hold the gaze, a spiral
of meditation and prayer.

Luxuriant chicory was growing
like an eye of water and sky
that opened to the final mystery

where they found my father
on the side of the road.

## ABUSE

A woman picks green beans, counts them,
weighs them, puts them back, the way

she chooses her friends, measures them,
tests them till they snap. She presses her nail

on pears till the skin gives, leaves a dirty moon
in the meat of the fruit that seems to recede

from touch like the shoulder of a woman
who was hit before, knows the cut of a slap.

She knows the pain of a mango
that has been probed, has turned to bruise,

juice bleeding into the skin. Snug in their crates,
avocadoes have learned to take the abuse,

expect the dissatisfied searching: tight,
not ready for guacamole tonight.

# VOICE, SILENCE, MEANING-MAKING

WHEN I THINK ABOUT ALL THE CLASSES THAT I'VE TAUGHT over the course of a forty-plus-year career as a professor and writing teacher, the first words that come to mind are voice and rootedness. I want my students to take a journey inward, to forge ahead against the fear of self-disclosure and failure, and drop the mask of an objective and externalized self, oftentimes a false academic point of view and voice. Whether it is creative or academic writing, I urge them to explore their own personal voices and stances and from that perspective write about what matters to them.

I begin each creative writing class with this idea of rootedness, whether they are introductory, memoir, or craft classes in poetry or creative nonfiction. I ask them to do one of the following freewrite exercises. "Begin with one of these generative openings: "I am..." or "I used to be, but now I am..." or "I awake..." or "I am rooted in..." It is striking how quickly students get in touch with their singular voices, in plural form, for they differ from work to work. But that initial exercise gives them the sense right away that they each have a unique voice/s as writers, and they should embrace the voices within. Their voices can range from an intimate one to an impassioned

*I want my students to take a journey inward, to forge ahead against the fear of self-disclosure and failure*

>

> social critic, to a sardonic commentator on life's ups and downs. They immediately realize after this first exercise that their job as writers is to explore topics and experiences that they feel connected to and want to write about—whether it is academic writing, prose, or poetry.

My next concern has always been breaking the silence imposed by the inner critic, by self-censorship, by the voices inside that say "I can't write," "I have nothing to say," "I am not a good writer." As Lynda Barry depicts in a wonderful graphic essay about her process, "Two Questions," there are two questions that obsess an artist or a writer: "Am I good? Does this suck?" And she suggests that these questions and the concern with how work will be viewed by an audience stifle creativity and create writer's block. These two questions plague most creative writers. In addition, they provoke a stance of silence—I can't or won't write about what most matters to me because there always is the prospect of judgment. I believe that this stance is more profound for women. In many of my classes, my women students talk about the silencing they've experienced in their lives, their trepidations about writing about their deepest emotions and memories, and their sense that writing in a woman's

*My next concern has always been breaking the silence imposed by the inner critic, by self-censorship, by the voices inside . . .*

voice still so many years after the second wave of feminism is taboo or at the least risky—a challenge that must be overcome. Therefore, I strive to find ways in creative writing classes to combat this sense of silencing.

Finally, in my poetry classes, to help students explore their many voices as writers, to help them open up and gain back what Lynda Barry calls in that essay, that "floating feeling," I create a persona poem exercise in the hopes that through writing in the voice of an imagined persona that they channel aspects of themselves. I give them examples that I have written that I have attached to this essay: "Clara Peeters Speaks: Still Lives" about a seventeenth century, almost forgotten, still life painter and "Io in Modern Dress," a poem about Io, the mythic figure in Greek mythology. In both poems I create an imagined life for these women and portray a world that rendered women invisible, voiceless, and powerless. In both poems, the imagined women speak out against a male-dominated world—one has agency, the other victimized. After I share my two poems with them, I give them selections from Anne Sexton's volume, *Transformations*, her persona poems for figures in fairy tales. They particularly like

*I strive to find ways in creative writing classes to combat this sense of silencing.*

>

> "Cinderella" and "Rapunzel." I then give them the prompt of creating a persona poem and monologue for a figure in a fairy tale or cartoon or character from a book that they have read. I also bring in lots of postcards of paintings and photos of people from *Humans of New York* (This is also available online.) and/or *The Family of Man* and other photography books and suggest if the first choice doesn't appeal then choose a different postcard or photograph and imagine a character who would be in that scene. Then create a dramatic monologue for that imagined character and persona. I ask them first to jot down some details that they notice in the work or the postcard or photograph. And then I ask them to create and jot down some facts about the character (age, gender, appearance, clothing, actions or gestures). After this brainstorming, I direct them to create a monologue in the voice of the imagined character. We share these as a class and comment on what draws us in as listeners, and then I ask writers to exchange poems and provide suggestions in drafting another version of the monologue. As a last step, I ask them to reread their personae poems and find a point of connection between their imagined characters and themselves. This exercise, which has worked well,

*. . . find a point of connection between their imagined characters and themselves.*

develops their observational skills, use of descriptive language, and obliquely enlarges their sense of voice, self, and perspective through imaginative leaps of character development. Students avoid the fear of vulnerability by channeling their selves into an imagined character, but they also come away with a fuller sense of their own subject matter, concerns, and voices as writers. It is a very freeing exercise.

Voice, Silence, Real and Imagined Selves. These are the lessons I hope to give my students. I want them to embrace their many voices as writers, combat the many forms of silencing they face, and explore the terrain created by their imaginations as they also learn genres, forms, and techniques of poetry writing.

*I want them to embrace their many voices as writers . . .*

# IO IN MODERN DRESS
## (About Lucien Freud's "Girl with a Leaf")

The spiked leaf pierces my eye. I was the one who saw, the one who
couldn't close her eyes at night. The one who peered through the
pane and saw silhouettes. Naked limbs strutting
away from me. I was the one who saw shadows of bodies and tasted
the salt and silt of dead seas

It was no different when he came to me, no different to see the
body of a man
who was a god. No different to be claimed by the razor edge of a
glance. A piercing
line of sight claiming by body my fate. The edge of the vine leaf
sparks a sharp pain.
A scratch against the white of my eye. My eye scarred, pulsed open
by this forbidden view.

I couldn't help but see. Seeing so much like possession.

Now as he clothes himself away from me, I imagine his naked
body, his white
limbs, his breath that forms clouds rain and fire. His back a sheen
of muscle
His words a shimmer of rivers. His body a universe unto itself.

I say nothing.

The edge of the leaf pierces and burns. I am tangled in vines,
pricked and plundered.
My body turned foreign. Unknown to me.

And all for a forbidden glance. My punishment for naked sight.
I am my own plague.

guilt
sense of own desire, not just taken advantage of

# CLARA PEETERS SPEAKS: STILL LIVES
(Active 1607-1621)

How foolish these men. They see garlic bulbs bruised,
lemons half peeled.
Skeletal fish stripped of their flesh, tankards tipped,
drained of ale.
They paint empty oyster shells, pomegranate seeds,
bursting forth from rotting skin
browned rose petals, tulips, carnations next to a skull.
I see spiked artichokes, leaves gloss green.
Grapes and cherries touched with sunlight. A warmth
inside out.
Yes, fish die—slick, slithered on a plate, scales still wet
with the sea.
Eyes glaring as if to say, "I know my place. My worth in
your world."
Yes, the peregrine falcon stares at his kill: kingfisher,
finch, a parrot.
A dread of colors. Reminders of the real. Yet for me
lustrous celadon bowls rest next to pink crab and
crayfish. Clustered not devoured.
A hunk of Gouda, a pewter tankard. No hints of a
dessicated world. Just my bearing, my sight.
My profile haunts. Reflections in a goblet, shadows in
wreaths of silver on a decanter.
A trace of myself in a claret glass.*
I smile, place my signature P in twisted bread. Just a
little secret.
His earthbound universe mine. This earthbound world
unbound.

*Clara Peeters inserted self-portraits in her still life
paintings. One of them had seven hidden self-portraits.

# VOICE, SILENCE, MEANING-MAKING

I DON'T MEAN FOR THIS TO SOUND OVERLY DISMISSIVE or wise-ass, but as much as I love to write about history, music, politics, I love editing more. Thus, my natural migration towards poetry and, obsessively of late, haiku. The fewer words for me the better. Maybe I stay out of trouble that way.

Or maybe it's sheer laziness. To the chagrin of many friends who egg me on to finish either of the two novels I've started, the first, *Tuesday's Assassin*, a sullen tale of a copycat headline-making serial killer and my rock 'n roll murder mystery *The Blonde with Blue Shoes* (Jack Maverick is the down-and-out-gumshoe hero), they lie side by side on a shelf somewhere famished and unfinished. There's a forlorn stack of short stories in a basement filing cabinet somewhere. Decades ago I wrote and performed with two bands: one punk, the Sic Pups, and the other, commercially viable but too, too prescient for these times, New Nervous Voice. (We lost our recording/distribution contract in the same capitalistic squeeze that Joni Mitchell and Van Morrison did.) But carrying around instruments, fighting with drummers, and miles and miles of nightmare wires just exhausted me to the point where I realized I could just carry around my notebook and read and write

*There's a forlorn stack of short stories in a basement filing cabinet somewhere.*

# *. . . if something ain't affecting you, then you ain't breathing.*

anywhere at any time. Which came in pretty handy for a guy with wanderlust and a lax work ethic working for a certain utility company before these ragged days of GPS and binary code crunching.

I listen for the street comic cadence. I think rhythm always. I look for new words to replace the worn-out excuses for language politicians, salesmen, and cable news pundits overuse then let the sound of the newfound word take flight.

As far as influences, if something ain't affecting you, then you ain't breathing. Charlie Chaplin. Kurt Vonnegut. Kerouac. Gracie Allen. Richard Pryor. Mickey Spillane. Dylan. John, Paul, George, and Ringo. Joni Mitchell. Tom Waits. Dean Martin, believe it or not, his delivery is flawless. Robert Hunter (is there anywhere a more beautiful poem/ lyric than "Ripple"?) Robin Williams. Robert Creeley. Kenneth Patchen. Denise Levertov. Mary Oliver. Basho. Motown. Vivaldi. Groucho, Harpo, Chico. Steinbeck. Coltrane. Mingus. Miles . . . Mom 'n Dad 'n peers. Of course, whatever dire times we happen to inhabit are prime fodder, too.

I've always approached scheduling Calling All Poets featured readings as editing a living magazine. It might appear

>

sensationally selfish or high minded at first (and yeah, I admit, there is that) but, like any editor convinced of their salt, I hope I know what I, and the creatively-charged community CAPS has become, want to read, feel, be inspired by, calmed by, pissed-off by—and assemble the schedule.

It took me a long, long while to integrate wholly into the idea of an open mic. Jim Eve (the founder of the Calling All Poets Series) has, for eighteen years and counting, insisted on it. But even in the best of times how long can anyone listen to a poet moan? Even the most decorated, most award-winningest drones on after a while. And an open mic? Wow! They can get long in the tooth real fast. But CAPS open mics invite and inspire both the novice and veteran, so the mix has added indelibly to the life of a living magazine. New readers, new voices, new listeners.

But it's not a solitary assignment. It takes input from everyone, whether they suspect themselves to be conspirators or not. Every featured reader brings their A game. This in turn challenges and engages the open mic-ers. New voices appear. Old names drop new. Everyone becomes an agent of change and outreach. Then along comes First Friday of the month and the magazine comes alive.

*But even in the best of times how long can anyone listen to a poet moan?*

MIKE JURKOVIC

## TOPEKA

I never did get back to Topeka.
What was the point? There was bullshit
in every direction. Just like here.
Up n down. Forward, back.
Horizon to horizon. Moon to moon
n Grandma's down eight fingers n falling
into her chili n chips as Pop Pop swears at Quick Draw
and little Lena gets off the bus n walks into
the dim lit, dimwit, gimlet, gin house that
only the brave defy. Which is why I'm here.
Hiding behind happy hour. My religion lost
and my faith failing fast. Each dark minute
hauling itself forward. Towards the water.
Towards the morsel. Towards the dead legends
I call my own and number myself
among. We jump off in droves.
The chasm yawning. The darkness rushing by.
The mothballed freighters
falling twice as fast.
*Just grow soldiers* they say,
reminding me a lot of what I heard
back in Topeka. Where prairie winds
blow rust and water mains burst
just like that. Just like everywhere else
neglected by its people. Dismissed as a political problem
when, in fact, it's a culture. A question of folklore
and the lack thereof. No present. No past.
No holds barred when it comes to demise
and the dollars it makes. Squalor. Contempt.
A breed I've indebted myself to. A ruined lineage.
Just like Topeka.

# HESITANT SUITOR

She sirens me into every room
to let our ragtime loose.
Bach rolls in, Chuck rolls out.
From a new nerve we wail
w/o contrition. The ride, bell-like,
conjuring swing from consonant drifts.

She calls me to free her song.
Atonal. Dominant. Total head.
Riff. Root. Rubato. She is in my blood,
scatting. I have wanted this music for so long.
Me at the piano but alas, I am a hesitant suitor,
w/o the gumption to challenge her fervor
born in the maple and falcon. We unwrap,
from elemental copper, new codes.
We hammer a new language.
Dancing ensues! The tip jar overflows and
the bassist lays out. It's all melody now,
as it should be.

SUSAN CHUTE

# EXCLUSIVE ON THE ELUSIVE POEM

IS IT MUSIC? RHYTHM? RHYME? ORDER? BREVITY? DECEPTION? IS IT AN ENCHANTMENT? Does it say something you never heard before, something you didn't know? Or something you always knew but could not say? Is it a question? An answer? Is it an amazing feat of derring-do, a high wire act? Is it a puzzle? A belief?

*At too many poetry readings, the only introduction to the poet is a list of credits.*

After 40 years chasing poetry like it's a mischievous child running from the babysitter, I still don't know where or how a poem lives. I want it to be my best friend forever, but it starts giggling and skipping away.

I know other people who know its address, though. In this world of connections, that's a pretty good start, so I hang out with those local people at a literary series I founded called Next Year's Words. As the founder, it's my job to introduce the readers. At too many poetry readings, the only introduction to the poet is a list of credits. Befuddled listeners are imperiously dumped from the commonplace of calculating how far they fall from the poet's feats of achievement into a foreign culture of exquisite expression. Better to go gently into that poetic sphere. So I start with a line from the writer's work and ruminate about that line and others and mention how

75

> they color my own experience, and what I know about the person, and compare and contrast maybe even confound, and hopefully, somewhere within, is a word or phrase prompting the listener to hear the poet's tongue more completely, more fully.

Some poets can describe how they write poems. I'm not one of those. Oh, I know—best words, best order; tell it slant; immature poets imitate, mature poets steal; keep a notebook; take a line for a walk; eavesdrop; stick to a form; revise; revise; revise—somehow I always bungle the recipe. But write I do, and the only way I can tell you about it is to treat myself as a writer at Next Year's Words, and write my own introduction. Here goes:

Count your amulets. Catalog your breath.
This is all you have. This is what you get.
—from How to Get to Where You Are

Looks like a part of a poem, doesn't it? The lines are short. There's alliteration—*count, catalog.* There's repetition—This is, this is. If it looks like a poem, it must be a poem.

**COUNT YOUR AMULETS:** Is poetry a form of magic? For many years, I didn't believe in magic. But haven't poems transported me, comforted me, made me

# To catalog your life is to define it

laugh, cry, made me alive? If that's not magic (if poems are magic). . . . So what other treasures, relics, charms, beliefs, prayers convince me that I live? There's the subject of some of my poems.

**CATALOG YOUR BREATH:** Cataloging? I know all about it; I'm a librarian. Cataloging is a relatively simple matter— just sorting, right? Wrong: The manuals that explain it are thousands of pages. To catalog your life is to define it: to pin down the essence of it, to find precisely the right phrase. Who can define exactly what a life is? Poets, that's who. That's why I revise poems. To come closer. Never there, but closer.

**THIS IS ALL YOU HAVE:** Some people write beautiful poems of the exterior, never once mentioning themselves. That's not me. I can only tell you what I've seen, experienced, thought. So love me or leave me—the "I" is always lurking about my poems.

**THIS IS WHAT YOU GET:** What is it that I have? Why this, and not that? Should I look to the microcosm of my scrubby small life? Should I ponder the macrocosm of national affairs, natural events, justice, grace—fate? Big questions! Break them into smaller parts. Poetry is where I try to pose questions—sometimes the uncomfortable kind.

This is what you get: a few of my poems. May they speak. May yours speak.

## SONG IN A YEAR OF CATASTROPHE
*After Wendell Berry*

Learn the dark, learn the dark, the anger, the shout The
dismissal, the incendiary glare, the insistence The wrong
way is the way you must right.

When music screeches through the doorway, When your
voice goes walking along the polluted river, When your
heart thumps against an unrelenting requiem,

Learn the dark, die into how you are denied, Love the
absence. Harden yourself against Lost friends, the ticking
clock, the idle endless night—until

It flies straight at you, the martineta, Irish bird, black
white belly, black pupil, But pinion of parrot and peacock,
brightest green.

This is the bird whose plumage is renewed while hung To
dry. This is the bird from the Bestiary whose smallest Part
is incorruptible, dead to the world yet alight, flying

A violet sky, stretching the clouds apart. Uh-uh, It calls,
rise up, go to the window, let the cold embrace Your small
part, holy shadow in the sublime world,

With mind that mediates, levitates, leaves the past To
burn in higher draughts, conspicuous, virtuous, flapping
In the breach of day.

SUSAN CHUTE

# HOW TO GET TO WHERE YOU ARE

You must run from your childhood
as if the stove is on fire.
You must leave things behind:
 the blue Mother Goose;
the confabulation of china dolls
in the crib by the window;
the harlequin piper fluting a tune
while other children dance away;
the spaghetti you slurp
from the chipped plate on the red formica table
with its metal apron like a belt around your throat.

You must run from your youth
 as if you escaped a house under quarantine.
You must toss medicines you were spooned:
the blaring bumps of Beatles songs
 that set you gyrating while your pimples pop;
the unearthly bleeps of aliens;
the harmonies of Christian campfires
 that fill your tongue with Bible stories
that squash your sex
 like a thick yellow butternut stew.

You must not squander yourself
in the sorcery of make-believe. While you
focus on the living room scene,
 the backdrop is flying out. While you
bathe the ballerina in apricot light,
the stagehands are striking the scaffolding.
While the master feeds you
 shiny pennies and pints of beer,
the stage door is being locked.

79

*variation* *Keep feeling surprised*

> Still you must run
past gothic churches with wheels of angels
and starry blue saints raising thin hands;
past libraries engraved with quotations
from books that have burned
You must race up the stairs to the room
where venetian blinds shatter the sun.

Clothe yourself in iridescent snakeskin
to shield your venom. Take up
the magnifying glass to amplify
your filmy eye. Sort
the picture postcards
your friends have sent.

Pick a painted elephant
to save your memory. Gather your fictions.
Preserve your degrees.

Pack a pencil. Remember your keys.
Don't forget your cellular phone
to call in your emergencies.

*pace change*

Count your amulets. Catalog your breath.
This is all you have. This is what you get.

Now continue. *short commands*

## ACCOMPLISHMENT

*Poets understand the organic, actively-evolving nature of language.*

I DON'T TELL MY STUDENTS QUITE THIS, BUT I THINK OF POETRY AS A RE-PRESENTATION OF EXPERIENCE THROUGH THE HUMAN EXPERIMENT OF LANGUAGE, an existential sifting for meaning in all these goings-on, and a quixotic, no doubt impossible, attempt to render the thing exactly and nail the truth by bending that language and those experiences in new and unusual ways. The idea is to render the thing just strange enough that the reader will actually work with it actively rather than waiting for it to come. Poets understand the organic, actively-evolving nature of language. They are involved in the making of it and have freedom once the general competence in writing has been achieved. First, writing students must become active readers of poetry. They must see language-making ideas within an aesthetic construction, a form, and how everything has been built into that form syllable by syllable, line by line.

Then they must be able to step back and see that it's never simply reduced to its form (its construct), such as a sonnet, and it's never completed or "whole"; it's not finite, as it continues to live and grow as it's read and interpreted. The poem becomes a living, breathing, deathless, organic entity generating itself constantly.

>

> I never "teach" or share a great poem that isn't alive and new to me each time, or where students themselves don't present a new way of seeing it through different eyes. I tell them to cultivate their strangeness, that is, not to be afraid of themselves in revealing their odd turns of thought and observation. Wed to experimentation with language—that is where originality in writing begins. I point out the mastery of grammar in professionals and urge them to learn it so as to manipulate it across lines and stanzas, to create powerful phrases and toy with words, making verbs of nouns, adverbs of nouns, inventing their own words. Poets make words because they know and love language. I tell them to listen to politicians and advertisers to hear it butchered, shopped from the cliché warehouse, double-spoken, meaningless, or at best, the old familiar language that we don't have to work with, lazy words from lazy minds.

I tell them to write with their ears, the beauty of the human song, syllables in consort, the rise and fall of the beat. What are they singing? In what mood? In what voice? How is the sound working with the meaning, the feeling? I want to forget myself and live there.

*Poets make words because they know and love language.*

*Pay attention to the world around you and know that today will never happen again . . .*

I tell them to retrieve their sense of wonder. Recall how the light from the sun strikes at every hour of every day; recall that feeling. Pay attention to the world around you and know that today will never happen again, despite the seduction of sameness, the comfort of routine, the addiction to habit. "Writer's block" is an escape hatch. "Inspiration" is a myth, the lie we tell ourselves. You have to work to get good at anything; you have to sweat. Make that your habit. If you dedicate a time to sit down and put word upon word, idea upon idea will follow; excitement will grow, and the end will come. With editing and refinement, sometimes, the joy of accomplishment will, too.

# GHAZAL IN THE DYING SUN

She padded across the room, stopped, turned white, said,
"I'm kind of freaked out. Are there really harps in heaven?"

I see a pair of jungle eyes that come with female skin
alert to breeze and calm, no clown-like wings in heaven.

Hafiz has drowned in wine; I'm drinking beer and visions
of the time I was another fruit on another vine to heaven.

There's a hero in the darkened alley, a child on the river
path. Sheep graze the paved street; goats, the map to heaven.

We pray to gain what gain will get when the get is the gain.
Our fathers love us before their fathers were born, in heaven.

Where there was love there was no self, only a beat and bass
line. Melody was the other. Song of one plus, of heaven.

Fill the daisy with a tilt of shade; fill the trout with a
taste for salt; pour man into woman with a longing for heaven.

"I don't want that," she said, "clouds and angels." Dennis,
you fool, tell her this foot, floor, pallid hour, this heaven.

published in *Crush Test*

# SHE'S SO BADASS IT HURTS

I. Magicicada

Spontaneous articulation in freedom
to exploit the dark of blinding
sunshine, the sweltering air with its
tangle of competing waves she emits
outward into ether, rebounded
back again from every surface of world –
the dented facets and crease and point
of ceaseless windblown sails of leaves
and needles green, block of trunks
and blip of bees; exotic warp of spaces
sing her to herself.

Crushed inside this ball of her own winding,
she senses in the pressure an overture
of soul: the Other? Incubus? Partner
to the song? The song is thus:
*my eyes see the mother of mystery*
*is beauty. My eyes sting; my eyes*
*are lashed and warped with shine,*
*involute in what I see, seek; I prism*
*the light through my wings: my wings*
*describe the inscape of my contour's cry.*

>

> Cracked her own shell to scale this big dizzy,
shed thirteen, seventeen years safe earthen niche
for the fearful glad risk of this beech,
to sing and fall into the arms of her song.
Whose song? lives one day
to sing among millions, dies myriad
deaths and launches again, thirteen years,
seventeen, every second, every century, sole
and collective. To the throng it sounds thus:
*Bleeding means. Bleeding means. Bleeding means.* No,
the drone of undifferentiated tug –

work, hunger, drug – not beauty, tendril
to the trigger love, container of the perfect origins,
the perfect return, O consummate moments!

II.   Tymbals

After the prime numbers of nymphs
in progress, safe from predation's even cycles,
she excavates into sky (saved from the paved
road and lot which entomb brethren's dreams).
Her torso serves – its own resonance chamber:
not the stridulated cricket rubbing of sticks,
but the membranous frequency of being,
the high wire belly dance of identity's tone.
Her fluted eyes fishlens the forest; nimble
limbs rememorize the twigs; iridescent
skin enacts the whiffle of the wind. Organs
translate the audited circuit, tymbals to tympana.
What would *you* say, stepping from your crusted molt?

III.   Instar

That's not what we have known? Only the male can sing?
You speak from the cradle of your crusted molt.
We call adults *imagines*. They say the first
haiku was a hermit painting grass on dew.
Hear what you see! invent the odor of emotion!
Function has delivered us beyond flight
to the new abyss and colony of maybes.
Wave to the old craft, the servile mass.

IV.   What I heard

Fingers of quicksilver light, the veil that reveals
all beauty in its liberating caul, longing.
I heard the sweet click of birth's secretions
(burst of berries, slurp of fruit in drip),
the stick of willful matter pressed in kiss.
A roar in the trees, the glow beyond the hill –
city nightlife ringing, or saucered empyreum
descending – the blacksmith demon's furnace.
He fashions magic cicadas who will master him.

published in *Fugitive*

## POETRY AS DISCOVERY

THE CRAFT OF WRITING POETRY, I
HAVE LEARNED, ASSUMES THE FORM
OF TWO SEEMINGLY PARADOXICAL
SETTINGS: one of freedom and one of
refinement. When I was working toward
my MFA in Creative Writing, I had the
pleasure of the late poet Leslie Scalapino's
tutelage. Influenced by Buddhism and the
Surrealists like André Breton, Scalapino
urged me to push beyond meaning and
beyond the recesses of my mind. I am not
certain I have ever fully comprehended
that teaching, but her voice retells that
lesson to me every time I am stuck in a
poem. When I was working toward my
PhD in Native American Studies, I had
the honor of being mentored by Nez Perce
scholar and poet Inés Hernández Ávila.
She told me that poetry for her is a place
of "total freedom." "Like a giant jigsaw
puzzle before you," she said, "it is up to
the artist to find where those edges meet."
The exploration that is poetry is one half
of the modes in which I challenge myself
to create. The other, refinement, is the
necessary dedication to sharpening and
perfecting language itself. This can appear
in many ways: collaboratively through
workshopping and poetry sharing, or in
isolation throughout draft after draft.
Efficiency may be one of the most accurate
ways to characterize poetry writing.

*The exploration that is poetry is one half of the modes in which I challenge myself to create.*

# "[Poetry] is a room to enter . . .

This paradox of expansion and contraction underscores the autonomy I have as a creator to keep those modes in suspension. It also implies mobility. If the poem is a place of discovery (the journey to find out where the edges of meaning meet), then I must move in a poem, and ask my reader to move as well. If I want to know something more deeply and more intimately, poetry helps me do that. Mojave poet Natalie Diaz (who is fast becoming one of my all-time favorites) says in an interview, "[Poetry] is a room to enter. There are thousands of ways to enter that room. I want to try them all." It is as much about movement (ways to enter) as it is about the destination (the room itself).

Allow me to provide here an exercise that I often share with my students on this lesson of discovery. First, I place several objects in the middle of a table. The objects do not have to have any relationship whatsoever between them. The more wild, the better. Each writer is asked to select a seat around the table. Instruct the group to use all of their senses: they can touch, listen to, and smell anything the want. Then, in any way they would like (e.g. in verse, in prose, in a list etc.), they begin writing a description of what they observe and imagine for

>

> five minutes. When the time is up, each writer will move to another seat at the table. With this new perspective of the objects, each writer continues to write for another five minutes. After this second go at it, the writers are reminded to involve as many senses as possible and to not censor themselves; "poetry is a place of total freedom." The writers then move to a third and final seat where they have two minutes to write. Upon completing the three bursts of writing, the participants have ten minutes to edit their writing in any way they would like. Finally, go around the room. Allow each participant to talk a bit about the process. For example, did it feel safe or did it feel risky? Did it allow them to move beyond what they saw (to "push beyond meaning") or did it provoke confinement. Did the different perspectives stimulate new "entries into that room." Additionally, if they would like, they can read their piece out loud.

*did it feel
safe or
did it feel
risky?*

1. Interview with Natalie Diaz in *The Creative Independent*.
Brandon Stosuy, April 14, 2017.
At: thecreativeindependent.com/people/natalie-diaz-on-the-physicality-of-writing/

## *forge outside the limits of what they see*

I have found that requiring the participants to change their vantage points urges them to forge outside the limits of what they see, as the objects on the table remain the same throughout the exercise. The writers are primed, then, to begin to incorporate attention and reflection into a body of writing. The meeting place, where observation and imagination reside, provokes creativity. This, in turn, leads to discovery. It doesn't end there, however. The exercise is just the opening of one of those doors. Now it is up to each writer to return to their poem-in-the-making with the charge of precision.

## SNAKE RIVER II

*looks like Snake + river* [handwritten annotation]

> Always moving toward home
> whether outbound
>         a push from bank
>                 hop in, stay low;
> whether back again                    arms full of good aches
>         scent of walleye
>                 almost too-low sun.
> It could be any day in your life
>                 or mine. Together this river story
>         weaves protocol and compass
>                 *kinnikanik* and Camels;
>                         holds the quiet sculling patterns
> where hands mimic older hands
>         revealing journeys across poplars,     spring flooding
> filling lives no matter
>                 oars sweeping down into the thick
>                         storied routes —
> the ones we've known by heart
>                         and tell ourselves in the calm
>                 of paired travelers.

## BONFIRE II

Breath guides
the trail in.

Fuse foot and pine needle.

Ground as keel
or compass.
Ancient foot traffic.

This earth body could be:
calendar
forecast
index.

Markers ahead        squint eyes.
See ancestor dispatch.

Spot Lady's Slipper
(could be moccasin flower)
amongst Tamarack.
                Another earth memo --
                wood for snowshoes.

Slender shape of White Spruce cones
open. Season about to turn.

Identify Basswood.
Remember cradleboards
or saw-toothed leaves to run
fingers along.

Point to clearing. Call back
forest language as we look for traces
of cupmarks, tools, messages.
        Signposts of tenure
or family records.

## THE WORKING POET

IF YOU WANT TO WRITE POETRY, YOU
HAVE TO LIVE FULLY IN THE WORLD
AROUND YOU which means knowing how
to waste time productively. That means
you don't go about with your head down in
your phone and spend every spare minute
of the day posting on social media, texting,
texting, texting. If you're sitting in the
doctor's office waiting room, put your
phone away and observe the other people
who are waiting. Eavesdrop. Waiting on
line at the checkout? Who is in front of
you? What kind of food are they buying?
Hear an interesting bit of conversation?
Write it down; you may use it later. Odd
bits of conversation are "little word gifts."
I overheard someone in an animated
conversation about a dude ranch, brag, "I
went swimming with horses." It became a
poem called, (surprise), "Swimming with
Horses" as I tried to imagine what it would
be like. Would you sit atop the horse?
Swim beside it? The poem describes a
nearly baptismal experience, and I had
great fun working on it. With your eyes
open, you see something—a dog, a train,
a homeless man—and the image pulls at
you until it finds its way inside a poem.
Poets feel a lot of guilt because we spend
lots of time looking at things, gazing
out windows, listening. Conventional
folk think we're lazy. But our minds are
actually trawling for imagery, juxtaposing
strange, disparate things, working at

*With your eyes open, you see something*

# You love striking combinations of words, overheard words.

describing how one thing reminds us of another because that is how we work at naming the unnamable. Call it idling efficiently.

*yes!*

Writing poetry requires an intense awareness of the outward that merges with the inward to become a poem. If you already write poetry, you love words. You love striking combinations of words, overheard words. Recently, the young assistant at physical therapy was telling me how she really wants to take a class in welding jewelry, but the last one offered was full and they are strict about enrollment because students are *working with live flames.* The image and its suggestive splendor gripped me. First of all, it's a fabulous title. It's also one hell of a metaphor for life, because much of life is dangerous and we get burned, more often than not. So, no, it's not a poem yet, but I have high hopes and it's in my journal which is where all possibilities should be duly recorded.

Also, don't ever discard something because it's ordinary or seemingly unpoetic. Case in point: I had to take my car to an autobody shop as I'd been rear-ended (probably by someone on his phone). The location was a dull, industrial two-story building down near the river. As I hung out in the parking lot while the

>

> proprietor inspected my vehicle carefully, I felt chilled on the dank December morning with fog shrouding the river, but at the same time I was overcome with the strange unexpected beauty of a few seagulls wheeling in the whitened sky, and as I gazed at my car, I realized that my husband had washed it and vacuumed it out the day before on another bleak and cold December day. The image of the homely place and the soft fog and my husband's deed somehow melded together to become a poem about love, and how real love is not the glamorous thing we make of it, but something so much more. It was totally unexpected, so it felt like a surprise and a gift of sorts. Now had I been scrolling on my phone, the poem, the moment would have been lost. Poetry is usually about the intensely ordinary made extraordinary through the alembic of the poet's vision. So, please, waste your time productively.

*Poetry is usually about the intensely ordinary made extraordinary*

RAPHAEL KOSEK

# SWIMMING WITH HORSES

is like nothing else: the heavy body
svelte and muscled entering
the lightness of water — blue tipping plate
            of the lake, melding with
an earthy beast, a steady heart, the healthy
fear like a jet tearing
            the night sky of your bones.

"Swim!" the trail guide yells. You slip
        off the horse,
            find the water yourself,
the under-thrash of hooves, equine eye
            that corrals you like God—
hands, legs slicing the wind-chop
of water. You've never been so
            water-blind in sun, scraping

up onto the glazed stones
of the far shore, cord in your hands, finding
            your feet and breathing
hard: Hauled up, emerging
as if for the first time, the trees
            waving, the sky bright shining.

published in *The Chattahoochee Review*

# SAMURAI SWORD

. . . a man was swinging a samurai sword
and I don't know if it came to me in the sludge
of sleep or the voice on the radio while the coffee
steamed and hissed but a man was swinging
a samurai sword while a staggered V of geese
fluted above me as I stepped out into the new day
with all the old anxieties, buttoning every button
against the wind while leaves tore round my feet
and the secret tide of salt pressed upstream
towards Albany in the great river grey and stoic
where it could go no more but return to the sea
and I understood that something would be pierced
because that is what happens when a man is swinging
a samurai sword but I didn't know what or who and when
but the river keeps flowing and the geese call
and the sun flames on the river like hot golden money
                    spending itself on the last day.

published in *Juxtaprose*

# THE SERIAL POEM,
## or How to Avoid the Blank Screen

*I would argue that the serial poem is good training for beginning poets.*

LIKE MANY WRITERS, I AM AFRAID OF THE BLANK SCREEN. But I am more afraid of the lyric poem that arrives like a flash of light, beautiful and singular, a shooting star of the imagination, there and gone with nothing in its wake. Maybe it's the secret fiction writer in me, the desire for narrative, a next and a next and a next until the poem becomes a world in itself. Or maybe I can blame it on my early education as a poet: my first poetry workshop was a course in the serial poem, and so perhaps I'm trained to it, one poem spurring another, the screen never entirely blank but bearing a palimpsest of the previous poems, texts I scrawl over and through. Whatever the case, the serial poem is the poetic form I am most comfortable in, the one that brings me back to the screen again and again. And whether it ruined me for the singular lyric poem or not, I would argue that the serial poem is good training for beginning poets.

I define the serial poem as a grouping of mainly lyric poems and passages (including fragments) that tend to interact as an organic whole. Some of the parts may work as stand-alone lyrics,  but they gain strength and meaning through their association with the other sections. The dynamics of the serial poem may be mainly emotive and associative,

>

> the result of strategic juxtaposition of separate poems and passages without a superimposed logical continuity, or they may operate based on a loose narrative structure, each poem building up the story like a chapter in a novel. In both cases, the object of the serial poem is neither to resolve a problem nor to conclude an action but rather to achieve the most open realization possible. The serial poem makes space for doubt, for digression, for reconsideration. The poem sprouts offshoots that become their own trunks, like quaking aspens, until what was once a singular thought or image is now a grove we can wander in, each part contributing to the complexity of the whole.

What I love most about the serial poem—and what makes the form useful for beginning poets—is that it encourages exploration. The serial poem asks us to develop and divert our thoughts, to push beyond what Richard Hugo calls "the triggering subject," that initiating thought that brought us to the page but which might, if we're not careful, become a kind of quagmire, our thoughts tediously circling the same point. Instead, the serial poem requires us to make the associative leap into new territory.

The other pleasure of the serial poem is that for writers who come to poetry from

*The poem sprouts offshoots that become their own trunks . . .*

# a night sky I can read my way across

fiction, it allows for a reconsideration of narrative possibilities. Many serial poems allow for a multitude of speakers and viewpoints: Mary Jo Bang's *Louise in Love* and Cathy Park Hong's *Dance Dance Revolution* come to mind, though there are so many examples. Unlike the short lyric, which is bound by its length to produce a single, unified utterance, the serial poem encourages the poet to incorporate the many fragmented voices of a culture, to wear multiple masks. It also encourages us to approach a narrative from multiple angles, to favor image over the mechanics of plot, and to leap from the long view to the keyhole and back again.

And maybe that is what I like best about the serial poem: while the shooting star merely passes through, gone almost before I can fully register it, those other stars stay behind, a night sky I can read my way across, linking star to star and finding new patterns, new narratives, in the juxtapositions of their lights.

> **HERE IS AN EXERCISE I HAVE USED WITH MY STUDENTS TO HELP THEM SPARK AND EXPLORE A SINGULAR LYRIC POEM:**

1. Take out a poem you've been working on that you would like to develop serially.

2. Choose a line from the poem and use that as the opening of a new section, writing from there.

3. Write a list of words (nouns, verbs, names, abstractions) that come to mind, for whatever reason, when thinking about this poem (either the original version, or the new section created under point #2).

4. Choose one of those words and define it. Think of ways it is used in the language: its connotations (both cultural and personal), its possible allusions, even its sound.

5. Select an image from an earlier section (either number 2, 3, or 4) and investigate it further in a new section.

6. Argue against an idea in the poem, or negate an earlier assertion.

7. Write three questions the poem raises. Answer one.

8. Repeat an earlier line from one of the sections and go in a new direction. Try using repetition of the last word of the line or rhyme or the connotations of a word in the line, for example, to open out the poem.

## FRESH KILLS

*Fresh Kills Landfill in New York, open 1947-2001,*
*was once the largest man-made structure on Earth, visible from space.*

Our kingdom is of trash

Trash the crown
of gulls wheeling on the methane updrafts

Trash the throne,
this scaffold of carcass and crust

Out of alley and attic, out of sewer and sluice,
trash creeps among us—

Trash the claw, the moving in darkness

Trash the animal out of place:
the body blown against the fence, the meat that spills over the border

Trash the skin we shed and shed,
and over it grows, and over it grows—

Trash the forest.  Trash the reef that whitens the sea,
that drags the sky, that flaps
its baggy wings in the branches of trees

Trash this language
that clutters, that eddies and snags, and whelps
its litter in hoarded places

Trash this mouth that undecomposes

This mouth now waiting to howl

CLAIRE HERO

# IN THE SKULL OF COYOTE THE WORLD, OLFACTED

I find the skull of Coyote
& put it on, & walk

into a city built of spice & stench—

.

Stench has built pavilions
under the stars, built warehouses,
built bridges. Stench has skyscraped

molecule by molecule, blood-engineered.

Wearing the skull of Coyote I walk
through this abandoned city.

There is alarm on the wind,
a door slams, fear manufactures
its empty prefabs—

There is my scent on the wind
& I follow it.  Wearing the skull
of Coyote I track my scent

.

to this hole, this one, where once
I knelt, where once I tossed in
pieces of myself – tongue & eye –

& listened for the sound when
they hit bottom—

where my scentghost listens still
for the echo—

.

Wearing the skull of Coyote I breathe.
I breathe myself back into myself,

small colony forming
on the far shore of this world.

x

# NURTURING NEW POETS

THESE TWO POEMS WERE WRITTEN PERHAPS THIRTY YEARS APART and illustrate how alike and unalike a person's work can be. At the time of "The Full Moon Illustrates" I wrote sonnets in false rhymes in meters that depended on the number of syllables per line. It depends upon the Greek myth of Salmoneus, but filtered through a play by the Dutch poet Vondel. The scenery is loosely based on Provincetown, MA.

"Mayan" is much simpler, four-lined trimeters, a background of Belize, depending on the remark of a man at one of the digs that mayan perhaps meant "I don't know," hence the loose refrain of the poem. The first lesson I learned for a poet is to read widely; read other poets, yes. If possible read poets in other languages. Read in history, philosophy, and theology; I am not learned in any of this, but it gives me my vocabulary. I suspect that in "The Full Moon Illustrates" I had been reading Yeats in his middle period, and that in "Mayan" I was reading late Yeats, as well as certainly Geoffrey Hill. In the summer I read Virgil, Dante, Goethe, or Joyce. And a poet should never stop looking back at childhood; it feeds the childhood deeply. As is obvious, my syntax is very loose; I pack the line, but I am ready to defend it.

*The first lesson I learned for a poet is to read widely*

ROBERT WAUGH

## THE FULL MOON ILLUSTRATES

The full moon illustrates gods
or statues, selfhood perfected:
avenues, backdrops give down to
the powerful lapse of the shore—

spadework: stones, figs, goldenrods,
precessions of zodiacs fed
out of reality ripen new
tinfoil divinity—clangor

assuming the nimble creation,
marble and petal and castle
of sand and the fall-away tide,

thunderbolts of implausible
properties; skies of the world slide
to a crisis of the prodigious sun.

## MAYAN

As for me I don't know
though god walks in the sun
in every courtyard we
cut from the green mountain,

god lurks in every hill,
his square brow frowning at
uncovery, his stone
paunch the home of the rat.

As for me I don't know,
though god works every fire,
every river and stone,
every skin, desire.

I cannot make him out,
god is the knob we find
today in the ancient root,
god is often blind.

God burrows in the hill
that grows upon him, god
bows his head down, god grows
by the rank sod laid on sod.

As for me I don't know,
something within my heart
lies hidden, no less than god
my god in counterpart.

## DELICATE TIGHTROPE

CREATIVE WRITING TEACHERS HAVE A
DELICATE TIGHTROPE TO WALK.

On the one hand, we want students to
feel free to express themselves through
the assignments we provide. On the other
hand, we expose our students to exemplary
models of good writing so through
emulation and revision they will hopefully
discover that ever-elusive voice we keep
telling them is so important. We want
them to walk out of our classes in fifteen
weeks understanding it's easy to peck out
stream-of-consciousness psychobabble
onto a keyboard; real art requires tireless
hours of crafting, frustration, and creative
decision making.

This is particularly difficult with poetry.

Each semester, my primary objective,
established in the first class, is to
challenge students' expectations of poetry.
In a sense, I seek to "de-program" their
previous misconceptions about poetry
being the aforementioned stream-
of-consciousness psychobabble sans
punctuation and capitalization. I work to
counteract the notion often unfortunately
taught in high school that poets supply
their poems with fixed meanings even the
most poetically-challenged reader should
be able to discern from pre-determined
multiple-choice questions.

There is a scene in the 1989 film, *Dead
Poets Society*, in which the late Robin

*real art
requires
tireless
hours of
crafting . . .*

Williams's character, Mr. Keating, a young, inspiring English teacher at a prestigious private school for boys, asks a student to read a vapid, sterile introduction to poetry in the class text.

According to the passage:

*"To fully understand poetry, we must first be fluent in its meter, rhyme, and figures of speech, then ask two questions: One, how artfully has the objective of the poem been rendered? And two, how important is that objective? Question one rates the poem's perfection; question two rates its importance. Once these questions have been answered, determining the poem's greatness becomes a relatively simple matter."*

The explanation then goes on to provide students with a scoring grid by which they should be able to quantify a poem's "greatness" based on its components.

Mr. Keating stands at the blackboard and draws the grid while dutiful students copy it into their notebooks. Then he turns to his students and says:

*"Excrement. We're not laying pipe; we're talking about poetry. How can you describe poetry like* American Bandstand*? Well, I like Byron. I give him a 42, but I can't dance to it."*

Keating then instructs his students to rip out that page, then the entire introduction.

I show this scene to my students the first class, and ask them the point Mr. Keating

> is making. We then read several poems I feel will challenge their expectations of "good" poetry, like Mark Halliday's "Dorie Off to Atlanta," Ron Padgett's sonnet "Nothing in That Drawer," and the opening paragraph to Herman Melville's *Moby Dick*, not "poetry" but definitely poetic.

During the semester, I require students to read poems both conversational and heavy in implications. I tell them poems are about things poets wish to share with the world. They are reflections on experiences, and we are walking along with the speakers sharing in those experiences with them. Once we know who is speaking to us, students are urged to allow the poem to speak to them, i.e., connect to something that jars emotion, memory, or questions.

*poems are about things poets wish to share with the world.*

All in all, I want students to understand that poetry is not concerned with figuring things out, solving problems, like in mathematics or science. Poetry is about contemplation and bewilderment. It's a force that unifies us in the frustrating conclusion that we are all mixed up in this mess together with the same questions, concerns, and fears.

Before it's their turn to write their own, I show students drafts of a poem I have workshopped. I photocopy pages from my journal complete with cross-outs, arrows linking sections, asterisks, and notes in

## *they need to consider how closely the intrinsic pattern complements meaning*

margins. Then I present a typed draft and several copies workshop participants have annotated, followed by a final draft reflecting those annotations.

When it's time for them to write, I give students basic guidelines. If they're going to undertake haiku, for example, they have to give me several, not just one. The same for limericks. If they choose a form, like a sonnet or villanelle, they need to consider how closely the intrinsic pattern complements meaning so they're not just writing something that sounds pretty but means nothing.

On the day their poems are due, we workshop. A student writer reads their poem aloud, then another reads it. We go around the room discussing it while the original writer remains a silent observer. The student is not allowed to weigh in, explain confusing parts, or influence another's interpretation until all who have something to say have spoken.

Their final "exam" is a portfolio containing drafts of their work along with a reflection on how their writing has evolved over the semester.

Students generally emerge confident. Some decide they want to be writers (if they haven't already determined that); some conclude they *definitely* don't want to be.

## COLUMBUS DAY

I like to think I become Atticus Finch
whenever my children inquire
about things they don't understand.

I don't want them to discover as teenagers
that the bad guys don't always lose
or that mommy and daddy aren't perfect.

So here I am watching the parade.
The fire department and the boy scouts
certainly are impressive.

Whatever it is rotarians do,
they sure know how to smile and wave.
There's the town supervisor and his council,

The VFW, and the county's oldest resident,
following the high school marching band
blasting out "America the Beautiful".

My daughter sees him first,
perched upon an inflatable Santa Maria,
the Nina and Pinta bringing up the rear.

"He discovered America!" she declares,
and suddenly I'm struck dumb.
Not even in the car home

do I inform her it wasn't the real Columbus
who winked in her direction;
nor did he do what her teacher taught last week,

unless the lesson was on European colonialism,
unless twenty-five first-graders added
to their vocabularies words like

"genocide", "intolerance", or "small pox".
I pull into the driveway still wrestling
with the notion of sitting her down

after dinner and revising the myth.
Instead, I send her off to bed later to dream
about the next celebration between
those bucolic pilgrims and the Indians.

## ONE KIND FAVOR I ASK OF YOU

The last to be buried here was in 1912.
According to her headstone, "Zitkala Humphrey"
was seventy-six, a "beloved daughter, wife, and mother".
She's here with both sides of a family
that stretched back to colonization
and predeceased her by at least a decade.

Further down the hill
looks like a Halloween display:
misaligned markers,
                    characters once
proclaimed in limestone        reduced
          to aphasia,      ringed in onion grass and sumac.

Willard Turner was either "aged eleven years"
or "owed eleven ears".
Might Agnes McElroy still
be among the living, as fetching
at 110 as the day she married
"Norman" beside her?

If I lift the stone lying at my feet,
I'm bound to uncover a cavalcade
of politic worms, earwigs, millipedes
in quiet congress doing whatever
it is subterranean arthropods do.
Unless someone beats me to it

in the next forty years, I could bring a fresh
face to this place.  My wife won't concede,
though, having already announced her intent
to be with her grandparents and eventually
her father.  We really should be together.
That would entail being first in my family

to eschew the ancestral ground,
which will no doubt piss off my parents.
I could ask my kids to scatter my ashes
over the Hudson River, thereby
almost guaranteeing nothing by which
to remember me by but a couple hundred poems

in binders, journals, some pictures.
Have you heard the urban legend
about Walt Disney cryogenically frozen
in an abandoned movie studio
with John Wayne? Interesting prospect.
I often wonder what this woeful world

will be like the day those anachronisms
thaw and toddle down Hollywood Boulevard
attempting to order coffee at Starbucks
or chat up aspiring actors/singers/models
whose significant relationships are now
solely digital. Gazing out at the world

that left them cold, I don't foresee myself
doing anything so desperate. Wherever
you lay me, kind people, is fine, so long
as you come by every so often to read
me a little verse, and, as Blind Lemon Jefferson
sang, see that my grave is kept clean.

## POEMS AS SOUND MACHINES

FOR THE LAST DECADE OR SO, I have been teaching Poetry Workshops at Manhattanville College in Purchase, New York. I've also served as a poetry manuscript consultant at the Palm Beach Poetry Festival for about as long. There is very little that I like more than discussing poems, whether they be written by the well-established or by students just starting out. For me, poems offer a kind of deep meditation that slows the world down and enables us to share what is most essential and most difficult to articulate about being human. The poems I am drawn to often create an intimacy between writer and reader, a shared emotional space. The topics and emotional tenor may vary greatly, but drawing the reader close is a constant.

*poems offer a kind of deep meditation*

I try to help my students understand poems as sound machines. If a poem is deeply moving, we get closer to that feeling, to the voice that speaks the poem when we understand the mechanics, the little screws and nuts that create the emotional effect. Even if we can't write as fine a poem, there is great pleasure to be found from this type of close reading. We examine poems line by line, image by image, word by word. We may read a poem like "The Colonel" by Carolyn Forché and discuss how the strong sense of the

*If a poem is deeply moving, we get closer to that feeling . . .*

horrific is created. In this particular case, the poem's horror is magnified by the very flat reportorial tone in addition to the disjuncture between the achingly beautiful imagery and its subject matter. For example, "Broken bottles were embedded in the walls around the house to scoop the kneecaps from a man's legs or cut his face to lace." In this particular example, "lace" is matched with shredded skin. And the verb "scoop", most often associated with ice cream, is rarely used in the context of dismemberment.

I find that poetry can sometimes give my students permission to talk about difficult subjects. For example, I have taught many poems from Marie Howe's book, *What the Living Do.* Some of the poems touch on sexual abuse of young children by their father. These poems have opened the door for more than a few of my students to write about such topics. I also think of her poem, "Practicing" which gives permission to young girls to express their sexual feelings towards each other. As liberal as attitudes currently are towards sexuality, I find my students, male and female, gravitate towards this piece and often write poems of their own on such topics.

>

> There are also poems that teach a love of sound and language. I very much ascribe to what Peter Perieira says in his poem, "Anagrammar." There is magic in language:

> "That if you could just rearrange things the right way,
>
> you'd find your true life,
>
> the right path
>
> the answer to your questions."

If the workshop is successful, the students help each other explore their truest selves. I try to teach students how to be empathetic and inquisitive listeners. I believe this skill will serve them well in whatever they ultimately decide to do with their lives.

*There is magic in language*

## ECHOLOCATION

The whales can't hear each other calling
in the noise-cluttered sea: they beach themselves.
I saw one once—heaved onto the sand with kelp
stuck to its blue-gray skin.
Heavy and immobile,

it lay like a great sadness.
And it was hard to breathe with all the stink.
Its elliptical black eyes had stilled, were mostly dry,
and barnacles clustered on its back
like tiny brown volcanoes.

Imagining the other whales, their roving weight,
their blue-black webbing of the deep,
I stopped knowing how to measure my own grief.
And this one, large and dead on the sand,
with its unimaginable five-hundred-pound heart.

*[handwritten annotations: "abstract, maker it into concrete noun, not just feeling, becomes physical mass"; "literal - whale"; "figurative - sadness"]*

## WHAT'S MISSING

I have been cut loose and orbit,

wild, am not in sync with any moon,

as when I was a child, though back then

I would not have known the force

of women, living in a single house,

our periods aligned like vases on a window sill,

would not have shown an outward quiet,

as after heavy snow, its buffering walls

as I rode the tunnels to work

or tended a sick child,

all the while a wrecking ball

swinging loose inside me.

And now, moon, you appear

like a mouth, wide open.

## INNOVATION AND BEAUTY JUNKIE

*The laughter that blows away death*

POETRY HAS ALWAYS BEEN A GREAT FEAST, with every writer bringing the most delicious dishes to the table. The feast is ever more beguiling the more we all bring. As Ron Silliman has pointed out, fifty years ago maybe there were 200 poets working in America. Now there are many, many thousands (who really knows how many) as the result of MFA programs.

The upside? The deliciousness is ever more beguiling. The downside? It's often harder to locate.

I'm old enough to have both written before and after the Internet. Pre-internet, it took me a long time to find my community. My moment came in finding Clayton Eshleman's important journal *Sulfur*. These days, there are no true gatekeepers. We can all start a magazine, print or electronic, a blog, tweet our poems and our friends' poems, bring poetry to Instagram, start a Tumblr, curate a reading series. Most of these things won't pay you, but that's okay. Late-stage capitalism doesn't value poetry, but the arts are what the great Frida Kahlo called, "carcajada" or the laughter that blows away death. There are loads of places to publish, but it's up to you to start your own journal if you don't like what you see.

> Before you send out your work, do your research both for yourself and your prospective publisher. You'll want to send to places that are a good fit. Don't send a scattershot of submissions into the universe. When I've been a poetry editor, I've always looked and hoped to find work I'd never seen before. I'm an innovation and beauty junkie.

Over the years, I've curated a couple of reading series and an online journal, collaborated with friends who are writers and visual artists and musicians. I am also president of an all-volunteer organization that has a visually and sonically unique underground performance space, along with our Annual Subterranean Poetry Festival. The more we bring to our community, the richer and more nourished we all are.

*do your*
*research*

A poet friend recently invited me to teach one of her college classes, so I got to work with a group of freshmen. Many of them had been reading poetry and writing poetry their whole lives (which impressed me), but they had very rigid ideas about what a poem is, and could be. Before the class, I asked that each student bring a short poem they wrote and hand it to the person next to them. On their laptops, I asked them all to type (one line at a time) a line from their short poem into Google

# I'm interested in the frayed edges of language

without quotation marks and search that line. They were to let their eyes run down the search results and pick out text that appealed to them, being mindful of that line between appropriation and theft, never clicking on any links. This is a great way to break out of our own habitual language. Once they had done this for a while, they constructed poems out of the found text. Then my friend who taught the class sent me some of their poems. She made an interesting observation: the students who were most rigid about their writing experienced the most freedom.

I'm interested in the frayed edges of language, what's possible when it's let loose, what language comes to tell us. When you become tired of yourself and your language, collaborate. Collaborate with other writers and across media. It will pull you out of your habitual language into new territory.

# SHE WAS AN INVENTED FORM OF LOVE
(after my own poem "Her Lilac Ovals Roam" – as suggested by Google)

Her biceps were both interactive and saved by rock and roll
Her space holiday was a like a copper wire lisp
Her Oklahoma had lucky pretty eyes
wore an organza made of oil and oval shaped screens
The mirrors rattled
Her profile roamed
The halls were ultra simple
She laughed by proxy
Her laundry fields were filled with lamb red meat
She bought her lacrimal bones over the counter
She was born with a lyric gland
Caviar dream font, caviarteria
She had an affair with codfish and ash, with Warsaw avocados, with
cigarette appetizers pumped with vodka
And also the trees as such
She could use the word "avarice" in a sentence
She was a totem to prodigality and covetousness
She knew that avarice cannot synchronize with cartoons
She can't tell the difference between Caravaggio and caramelized
onions
Her sea salt is gluten free and from Montana
She was an invented candy of illuminati informed intentions
Her hands were rescued by an oracle
She makes casseroles out of war
She has a continuous lean toward miracles like a a blind glass or a
carat of gold
Her camels, her china, her facts diagrammed
She fishes in financial Egypts, her pool is filled with caramel
Christ in school prayer with cheese please
She is capitalized in cat-like tread
She is a cleverbot and an international rose celebration
She makes the saints run to windows and head bellyup to the sky
She sailed accountancy through bloody seas

ANNE GORRICK

*Complexity of thinking about people in diff way*
*weird pairings, strike new*

She is more cowbell than half marathon
Her volatility awaits the treasure market
She has vivid dreams in Port of Spain
She will be remembered for giving in
She wonders if texturizers are better than relaxers?
Which is better, beer or god? —
She conducts her relationships in quotes —
She is an emissary to relic castles
Her jacket is celestial
Her body is carved out of sandwiches and crushed Portland —
She plays rabbit babysitting and rabbit dress up
She sings coffee songs and hangs thermal lined curtains
She is a confusing summary of no homework and cracked bones ——
There is poverty behind every crime, and crime behind every
fortune
Chicken meat cheerleading, a voice full of money
Vanished grace, she is a bureau of adjustments ——
The amount of surface runoff increases the amount of light that
enters the eye
filtering a violent and flammable world
Poets in a telephoned abyss, reclusive
Someone made her out of reclaimed lumber, storm horses,
tailhooks
"You can build your own malice," she said like a malingering ——
eclipse
Her vodka vocabulary over glaciers, stochastic
She has Stockholm syndrome and a stocked pantry
She practices extreme etiquette
Her movements echo with ecclesiastic approval
She was made from scratch —
She is clairvoyant, sleeps late and snores
She points her claddagh ring at people
Her clavichord rivals a crock pot

>

> She was a milk experiment in Maine and an oral history
She wonders what an orange traffic sign means
Her oracle bone was wrapped in white paper
She was also an oracle of modernism in ancient Rome
Her planting instructions involved the Super Bowl
She went to the cemetery where Al Jolson was buried
Her root cellar is filled with camel spiders
She is an orange mild cigarette
She is entirety in its simplest form —
The velvet grip of her vein idiom, she is structured like cilia
She orchestrates Ravel like an Olympic horse
Hers is an aspen-feathered dress
Her verbs are metaphors for freedom
She is an adaptation in bats
When an object freely falls it is an imperfect actor on the stage
She is an orienting response
Nest myth, fabric, symbol, birdhouse
Her address is in a bird park
Tiger informally, orange month oil or bluejay egg
She is an aquamarine herbicide
The mummies in her coat are so warm, they're on fire
She formed the "I am here Coalition"
Coalesce, clamshell buckets, narratology
She wants a meaningful life filled with new architecture
She is cloud agnostic
Her clover necklaces a clown fish, clover grows in her grasses
Grass grows over her vibrating concrete
Her viability replicates definitions
She is in a nondividing state, a laboratory manual —
Reed mystery triptych, the whorehouse quintet
Keith Richards is an essay in human understanding
An element occurs as a mixture of isotopes —

## ON WRITING POETRY

*POETRY.* FOR THOSE OF US WHO MAKE LANGUAGE OUR ART, THE VERY WORD IS A SOURCE OF POWER. IT IS OUR PULSE, OUR BLOODBEAT.

The best poetry begins in the body. Living pulse, real bloodbeat. Breath rhythm. Words come together; ideas and feelings form. Metaphor emerges as the most elemental music.

Donald Hall talks of "goatfoot, milktongue, twinbird": pleasure of movement, pleasure of sounds in the mouth, pleasure of knowing one can shape them. Yes. The essence of creating poetry is to leap into language, dance with it, make it one's own and the world's. Moving itself, it moves others.

*Metaphor emerges as the most elemental music.*

Here is a way to approach making poetry. Recall an experience. Let it flow from your head into your body until you know fully again what is now memory. Open all your senses: see, hear, smell, taste, touch again what you lived. Focus on one moment. Feel it completely. Do not try to understand it yet. Tell about it. Let the words come. Are they questions? Answers? Write so that readers and listeners respond with their senses, so that they let their bodies think. Do not explain; reveal. Let the images you create work for you. Ask the poem to talk, silently and aloud. People will listen and hear.

>

> Only such poems are poetry, the art to which people turn when they need to live again the stories, old and new, which give us the significance of life. Rhyme may be a part, form may be a part; but they are not the poetry.

"Make it new," said Ezra Pound. He meant take the deep and shape it wide, love and death and laughter. Take the sun which everyone knows and craft from it startling rainbows, light and color people need in their sky.

Do not bring everything—all sense and meaning—to us, but make us reach for it. Make us want to. Delight. Above all, write *real*; all our lives depend on it.

*take the deep and shape it wide*

## MY WRITING PROCESS

Poetry has been my core since I was 15 years old. As a full-time college teacher since age 22, early on I learned to write in "stolen moments," using concentration to make the space around me necessary for creation. Usually a first line arises and I continue, sometimes able to write it down immediately, sometimes having to memorize what I am composing until I can get it onto paper with a pen. (Only ONCE did I attempt to compose a poem on a computer, and it was a disaster.) I

*I believe strongly in the importance of reading aloud what has been written.*

write often and keep my first drafts in small spiral notebooks—I'm in my 83rd now, with nearly 8,800 poems (as of February 2018)—not worrying about how good they are until I move to the next step of deciding whether or not they are good enough to type into my computer and try to publish. Many, of course, never make it off the written page! I am fond of writing in small groups with others, prompts provided, and I believe strongly in the importance of reading aloud what has been written. (My doctoral dissertation for Northwestern University, where I studied Interpretation in the early 1980s, was *The Writer as Performer*, an ethnographic study of why writers read to audiences, how they read, and why people come to listen.) I agree with Gary Snyder that the role of a poet is to serve as a shaper of *communitas* and with Marge Piercy that a poet's work should be of use to others.

## LEADING WORKSHOPS

Bringing poets together to create and share new work has always been a priority for me. As soon as I moved to Ithaca, New York, in 1975, I organized a weekly reading circle and then joined the emerging Ithaca Community Poets with its

>

> grant-supported readings and workshops series. A few years later I began to teach for, and went on to direct, the national Women's Writing Workshops founded by Beverly Tanenhaus, which became the Feminist Women's Writing Workshops, Inc. My ethos is to encourage poets to share the truths they need to share, with language that communicates clearly and surpisingly, working away from easy, stale cliché to words that join together with strength and beauty. I bring this ethos to all of my teaching, and I am happy to report that many writers of varying ages have flourished from it.

*working away from easy, stale cliché to words that join together with strength and beauty.*

KATHARYN HOWD MACHAN

## PEARSALL PLACE

we poets live
on the edge of wild,
ordinary people
who ask questions

why does blackberry
blossom white, stain purple?
where does cardinal
build a fire against snow?

we walk this street
past the Dead End sign,
toward the sound of gorge
stream pulsing silver

when does silence
begin and end?
what can sky say
to morning mushroom?

*good wild sacred*
Snyder tells us
entering the ordinary
temple of the world

who am I touching
egret's still flight?
how do I carry
voice from this green?

first appeared in *Anima*

# RATS

*for Seth*

Don't put them into every poem.
Don't let them dance their dark thin tails
into how you choose your language
*A* to *M* to *Z*. Dismiss their eyes.
Forget how your brother's fingers

nested in your every nightmare,
slinky skin and pulsing movement
forbidden, forbidden, forbidden.
Rats, after all, are best
hung up in dead witches' cellars

with black scarlet-patterned bodies
of spiders he threatened you with.
Don't write about it. Don't write
at all: just read and read
old fairy tales

and when you find the one that calls
for dancing slippers made of glass
slam the book shut with a thud
before you learn about the coachman
starving for a fairy's love.

## TO WALK THE PERIMETER OF WORDS

# I used to read the dictionary for fun

MY CHILDHOOD FRIEND from the days of Asbell Elementary in Fayetteville, Arkansas, sent me a message a few years ago, reminding me that I used to read the dictionary for fun in the fifth grade. I had forgotten this habit. But when reflecting upon it, I realized that I had, in fact, never stopped reading the dictionary for fun.

I often scroll through the *Oxford English Dictionary* online searching for words I don't know (so many) and those I think I know. What remains hidden? Their etymologies? The multiple denotations? Their age and associations? Their various forms?

It was A. Van Jordan's poem, "afterglow," from his book, *M·A·C·N·O·L·I·A*, that first called my attention to its dictionary entry-like structure. The poem uses different images of the word "afterglow," beginning with an image of the Ohio sky at sunset. It ends suggesting the flushed faces and bodies after a romantic liaison. Its prose block structure is used to contrast and play up the lyrical repetitions and intimate landscape. The poem's sonorous and imagistic travels captured both my pedagogical and writerly imagination, and I began to assign it along with what I call the "O.E.D. poem" as a first exercise in nearly every poetry workshop I taught.

>

> In this assignment, I ask students to consider the varied approaches to an individual word. They look up the multiple definitions of the word that they choose, along with investigating its linguistic history. Often, they are surprised to find that the history of the word "sad" came from the same root as "sated" and so meant "enoughness" before its gradual transition to "melancholy."

*wav*

*look up
the multiple
definitions
of the
word . . .*

As part of their pre-writing exercise I ask them to explain why they chose the word and what associations they bring to it. Is their choice based on special letters (*q! z!*)? Does it have hard consonants that satisfy or contrasting short and long vowel sounds? (*gut! paprika! dazzling!*) What are its connotations? While words often have public connotations because of TV, literature or historical events, I have found that it is often a student's personal connotations that inspire surprising, poetic leaps.

*mix up*
*a word*
*with*
*other*
*words*

Other times, it's what the word rhymes with ("widdershins" with "Wonder Twins") or the words that a word contains ("gorge" and "us" within "gorgeous"). Or the way we mix up a word with other words so that the relationship we have with it becomes more familial, more complicated. Each word is bound up and mixed with sound, sense (or nonsense) and suggestion.

In my own *O.E.D.* poems, I have found that archaic or obsolete words often launch me into the surprise of the unknown and into narratives, research, and reflection. Words like "escapeful" or "namecouth" encourage me to tap my own experience and thoughts through the shape of the word and the worlds it contains.

## NAMECOUTH,
(adj.) known by name; well-known, famous; notorious *(rare).*

Let's say Maurice the Pants Man or
 Rizutti's Good Night Café what used
to be Old Billy's Lounge now charred

on Millbury Street down from what was
once Stony O'Brien's where your Gram
used to sit with her boyfriends into

her 60s, drinking gin & giving
you & your brother & sister
quarters for the jukebox, now called

Nick's (cuz Vincent & Nicole are so
in love, says Captain Bob).  Let's say
the Greyhound that used to be

Rafferty's & before that a name
I can't pronounce in Gaelic & where
they say the Baker was blown & shat

that girl & I wonder which corner
or john & how much stench that place,
that dark place where we all go to watch

the World Cup with Richie Scales,
Allie Bombz, Bells & Whistles—
*Everyone*, you tell me, *has another*

*name or several, better known than
their own:* Giant Jesus & Baby
Jesus, Husky Jay & Bakery Joe,

Trojan Mick & Pacman Pat, Lord Pork,
Fat Ron, Polish Stosh & the Warrior.
Even in Texas, Michael mentions

"the Vernon" to Sue, his liquor
store gal from the Woo, who gives him
the thousand mile stare.  She says,

*Bucket o' Blood & We were told
to look away, cross ourselves
& the street when passing that place.*

Published: *milk* (fall 2015)
and in *From the Hotel Vernon* (Salmon Poetry Press)

## ESCAPEFUL
(adj.) *Giving a chance of escape.*

Makes me think *baleful/ grateful/ pitiful*— that window in
Joplin, Missouri
at 17/ a wishful transom /that led to the roof behind the
honey locust where I went/ dreamt *away* as if it were its
own country/Country of *Not Here*/ where I was then
in that age of *me:* grazing desire to light out from that
grayed-in mining town—
"the city that Jack built" / Jack being zinc & sink holes
dotting 35.6 square miles from Range Line Road to
Soul's Harbor to Crystal Caves /filled in for a parking
lot/ where Bonnie & Clyde holed up in the 30s/played
rummy, chain-smoked Camels/ robbed, killed, fled/
left behind a film-filled camera the *Globe* developed:
Bonnie's Mary Jane poised on fender/ Clyde holding her
in a bride-over-threshold pose /or that shot with arm
akimbo and pistol, / hip cocked & cigar at lip. / While
skirting
the edges/ of Bienville Parrish, their ambush/ *turned
circus-like*/the coroner said, /throngs gathering to cut
the bloody locks from Bonnie's head, / Clyde's trigger-
finger and ear, /gather shell casings and shattered
glass from the Ford V-8/ sold as souvenirs. /Something
I thought about in passing /that Sunday we strolled
through Poreč /after mussels and schnitzel/ past that
fourth century church/ its marble from the Sea of
Marmara /an old Christian hideout/ its bell tower a
lookout/into
a western blue. / There were candles to light, gelato to
try, baseball jerseys for sale/ hanging from rafters in the
shops:/ *Bonnie #1, Clyde #2*


published in *Crab Creek Review*

# THE MOST COMPELLING WORK

AT SLAPERING HOL PRESS, for the chapbook manuscript that wins the annual Slapering Hol Press Chapbook Competition, the editors, Jennifer Franklin, Peggy Ellsberg, and I search for the most compelling work based on a holistic and eclectic vision which includes meaning, spirit, and art. In the history of the English language, the words "shaper" and "maker" were synonyms for "poet." What the poet shapes is a container for a refined linguistic expression of truth, different from prose narrative or dramatic literature. The greatest poetry tells a truth—about the spiritual world, dreams, visitations, the souls of the dead, or enlightened communion with nature.

Craft—the shaping and making of the creative container—is critical. At poetry conferences, some poets attend talks about craft, but craft and artifice are useless if the poet has no truth to communicate. The poet must write out of passion and necessity rather than to showcase the latest craft trend or fierce lexical play, which means nothing without meaning.

Poetry should inhabit a wider field accessible to general humanity as it has through most of human history. Relegated to the university and coteries, many poets today are like twins talking to themselves in artisanal languages comprehensible only to each other.

As the founding editor of Slapering Hol Press, one of the oldest chapbook presses in America, I have developed the view that there is no easy formula to determine what constitutes the best chapbook. In my experience, a body of poetry, well-shaped and well-made, which communicates something fresh and true deserves the attention of the widest possible audience.

Denise Levertov exerted the greatest force on my life and inspired me to become a poet. When I entered Harvard as an undergraduate, I was an alienated, idealistic adolescent with rebellious instincts. After cross-registering at MIT and getting accepted into Denise Levertov's poetry workshop, I encountered a

> set of paradigms that would change the course of my life. As co-editor of my high school newspaper, president of my senior class, and as someone who mainly expressed myself artistically through photography, I had never thought of myself as a poet.

Denise was a role model for me and many others in the MIT workshop. If I had not taken that workshop with her, I would never have become a poet. She instilled in me the belief that I could write a poem and contribute to the poetry community. At the time, I was also involved in the anti-war movement, attended many demonstrations and was arrested during the Harvard Strike. A group of us from the MIT workshop including Ernie Brooks, long-time musician, and Mark Pawlak, long-time poet and editor of *Hanging Loose,* formed the Mass Ave Poetry Hawkers and stood on street corners on Mass Ave and handed out poetry.

Visiting us in Maine and staying with us when we lived in D.C., Denise remained a close friend of my husband's and mine and corresponded with us until her death. Her views on the life of a poet, the poet as witness, the poem as prayer, all combined with her boundless energy, her unforgettable laugh and sense of wonder, her anger at injustice, and her light and airy humor indelibly etched her spirit on our lives. Denise read for The Hudson Valley Writers' Center, and she served as a contest judge for Slapering Hol Press. As she pointed out, the poet must be the medium through which the poem comes forth, and the poet must also allow the poem to take on a life of its own.

After realizing how few people read or comprehend poetry and how difficult it is to get one's poetry published, I became interested in creating publishing opportunities for emerging poets. My first intention was to found a press, but I never discovered any grants for small, small presses. In 1983, a grant of $3,000 from ArtsWestchester (then named Westchester Arts Council) allowed for the beginning of the Sleepy Hollow Poetry Series which later morphed into The Hudson Valley Writers' Center. It would take ten years of planning before it was possible to found Slapering Hol Press, the Center's small press imprint.

When I first proposed the idea of the Slapering Hol Press "Conversation" series, I already had Elizabeth Alexander in mind for the first "master" poet who would choose an "emerging" poet to appear in the same chapbook with an interview at the end. Alexander was a good choice, and President Barack Obama would follow our lead to choose her for his first inaugural poet after we published her "Conversation" chapbook. Alexander and the emerging poet she selected, Lyrae Van Clief-Stefanon, decided on the title, "Poems in Conversation and a Conversation," which became the heading for the whole series.

Rather than imposing our own standard for what comprises an "emerging" poet, the SHP co-editors decided to allow the master poet to create her own definition. Because we realized that opportunities for women poets still lag behind that of our male counterparts, we decided to limit the series only to women poets. This is a women's own series, one that provides space and time for women to show how valuable their relationships are to each other as poets.

Second to none, the most exciting aspect of serving as the SHP founding editor is the possibility of providing a small stepping stone for emerging poets and to mark the growth of their careers after the publication of their chapbooks. Along with the annual Slapering Hol Press Chapbook Contest, the "Conversation" series has allowed us to broaden SHP's impact not only by sticking within our mission of encouraging emerging poets, but also by providing another avenue for discovering and showcasing the mentor/mentee relationship for women poets. For this series, the poems themselves, and the interview at the end, give the reader the opportunity to understand the poets' writing processes and some of the issues inherent in their writing.

# IDIOT'S GUIDE TO COUNTING

How do you become one
with the horse, riding and becoming
the act of riding,
and the horse becoming the self
and the other at exactly
the same second, counting strides,
counting muscle movement,
counting fences, hurtling over
them with the horse, counting
the everything
of one?

How do you count, how do you
pull a muscle turning over
in bed at night—measurements
that change everything, counting
back to everything, the everything
of one, the pulled muscles of the back
of one, the entanglement
of one, the waves of particles
counting back, the quantum?

How to become one with
the branches of a tree, a grandfather
tree in an apple orchard
that no longer exists?
Separate one
from tree, horse,
counting numbers, counting
the grandfather tree
to find the solution of
one.

Counting trees, leaves, counting
everything as no longer
existing, counting
trees as one with the everything
that no longer exists.

First published in *Blackbird.* Also in *The Lunatic Ball,*
Kattywompus Press, 2015.

MARGO TAFT STEVER

# MY MOTHER IS DYING

In the place where she belongs,
suffering erases itself, doves
bring her seeds, horses sleep
next to her in the straw,

> where she belongs; a welcoming
> place holds her, keeps her
> from running away—the green
> greenness of the hay turning to gold.

Already, the rain's restless
trajectory. My mother is busy dying;
she no longer knows my name.
This is the wind of Eden,

> the wand of change, the last slave
> of silence, the knave of rain, so quiet
> the roving of each vacant quest. Let her
> be buried in the sea by the seaberry,

the briar rock, the fossil chamber.
Alone, blown, roadside stray,
the flown restless wayward ringing,
bells clang, ocean downcast, rolls.

> Wandering once again, now I
> return to the center, searching
> the level earth, calling her name,
> remembering that I am lost.

MARGO TAFT STEVER

The path unfurls before my dog
and me, walking to the rocks, the ocean
on one side, the bay on the other,
eiders blessing the waves.

        The seagulls' spontaneous burst,
        how it hurts with the radio blaring.
        My mother is dying, gone from
        a body that has abandoned her.

Cry because everything goes haywire,
because this is Apollo's siren lyre, the field-worn
answer, the childless response, children waiting
for some god to bring them home.

first published in *Poetry Flash*,
and in *CRACKED PIANO*, CavanKerry Press

JOANN DEIUDICIBUS

## *FOR JESSE, WHOSE WORDS STILL SING.*

The rendering of a moment as it unfolds in time; the essence
of an object or experience in concrete language that makes
the mundane once again new; inhabiting the senses through
verse; a literary utterance on the spirit of our time; the pleasure
of linguistic and imagistic patterns in rhythmic lines; the
quintessential music of syntactical and semantic spheres; the hum
and resonance of all that has come before and all that will continue
to be: all this and more, is poetry. I often turn to the *Defence of
Poetry* by Percy Shelley, who states, poetry "awakens and enlarges
the mind itself by rendering it the receptacle of a thousand
unapprehended combinations of thought. Poetry lifts the veil from
the hidden beauty of the world, and makes familiar objects be as if
they were not familiar: it reproduces all that it represents . . ."

There is, of course, no way to impart all of this to students in
a short, five-week, one-credit Understanding Poetry seminar,
such elevated abstractions or mysteries. We spend the first class
discussing our preconceived notions of the genre, considering
which of its characteristics distinguish it from prose. For
guidance, we look to the great poets' definitions, noting that
even these experts cannot agree though their words offer some
parameters. Ultimately, if the students can come to their own
evolving definition of poetry, if they are willing to give poetry the
time of day, to turn to it in the darkness, to listen to its buzz and
beat, then that is success.

All this is too lofty, though, isn't it? It lays an untenable burden
onto poetry's shoulders. How can we affirm this feared and
misunderstood genre within but also beyond university (where
even English professors have to defend it to colleagues)? In
addition, what use do we have for poetry in an age of blue screens?
Many think of poets as a wan bunch, antiquated with feather pens
and flimsy livelihoods. Poet stereotypes such as "a loony, a misfit,
a dreamer" don't help, either (Zavatsky 1-2).

Luckily, I did not know much about it when I came to poetry. Like most children, I had what my mother read to me, then what I read by nightlight after bedtime: nursery rhymes, Dr. Seuss story-songs in tightly knit metrics about green eggs and ham, Disney books, and the relentless repetition of a children's Bible. I loved singing along to records, so poetry's bouncy sounds attracted me. Soon enough, I was reading and reciting poems for a school contest in the third grade. I won a second-place trophy that is now long gone, but one of the poems, Frost's "Stopping by Woods on a Snowy Evening," I still know. (A poem that speaks to, or for you, will often stick to you.) Later, I was reading Dickinson, Hardy, Bogan, Cummings, Bukowski, Harjo, Espada, et al. I was writing poetry, and joined a group that would read at coffeehouses and bars. I was in a poetry club my first year of college. Then, I met professors like Mindy Ross, Jan Schmidt, and Pauline Uchmanowicz who encouraged my curiosity in artful, polysemic lines. Their classes reminded me of what Anne Sexton, one of my favorite poets, imparted to her students: that poetry is shaped largely through selective imagery and telling, sensory details, by intuiting "what to leave out" (Sexton & Ames 335). What's unsaid, the space on the page, the silence suspends us. There we might reflect and fully feel the currents in stillness.

What is more concrete than a poem, more measured? William Carlos Williams maintains that there are "No ideas but in things," ("About William Carlos Williams") and Ezra Pound before him warns, "Go in fear of abstractions" ("A Retrospect" and "A Few Don't's"). Pound submits to his own dictum in the 33-line-turned-3-line poem "In a Station of the Metro," where the blurry commotion of transitory faces in a subway station transform into pale petals stuck to a wet tree branch. This imagist moment—ephemeral features, the stark contrasts of light against dark, and the juxtaposition of the industrial with the natural—creates

>

> a striking snapshot. My poem "First Snow" attempts imagistic compression in short lines:

> Storm silence slows
> Slim veins of water, stills

> branch sway, weekend rush.
> Banks rise: bodies breathing. (3-6)

The poem conjures the quiet of a snowy day, where weather stops us from our business, causing us to reflect. Returning to Shelley's argument, poetic lines can reveal "the hidden beauty of the world" that we may otherwise be too busy to notice.

Archibald MacLeish provides complementary instruction in "Ars Poetica" that "a poem should not mean, / but be" (lines 23-24), placing emphasis on inhabiting description as opposed to offering prosaic exposition. Poetry's condensed language demands that every word works. Samuel Taylor Coleridge asserts that prose is "words in their best order," while poetry is "the best words in their best order" (Mills). The arrangement and unfolding, the multiple layers of meaning and word play, the furthering of poetic argument through the symbiosis of content and form—all this requires indefatigable revision. Poetry is all in the details and the timing.

What about the visceral, physiological response that poetry evokes? As Emily Dickinson says, "If I feel as if the top of my head were taken off, I know that is poetry" (Spengemann & Roberts). There is some suspense as a poem unfolds, as we expect something unexpected to occur. Current research published in *Social Cognitive and Affective Neuroscience* by Eugen Wassiliwizky confirms the chilling effect that poetry has on readers or listening audiences, even when the content is not macabre; essentially all the study participants experienced internal chills, while forty percent had visible goosebumps (Delistraty). Even more striking is that poetry induces a specific neurological reaction—engaging particular parts of the brain not prompted by other mediums such as film or song. Musicality is clearly essential to poetic language, but songs and poems are distinct. Wassiliwizky concludes that the "poetic lines that most emotionally stirred people were the most memorable for them later." Surely musical language enhances poetry's indelible impression.

In the Understanding Poetry class, created by Dr. H.R. Stoneback, I begin with Billy Collins's poem "Introduction to Poetry": the speaker comments on the antagonistic rigor with which we approach the genre, the way we train students to attack the text like a hostage, or "tie the poem to a chair with rope / and torture a confession out of it. [. . .] to find out what it really means" (lines 13-16). The compulsion to make meaning is common among us. Academics may find it difficult to sit in unknowing, or to admit to those we are supposed to provide answers to that perhaps there are none, or not only one. Poetry taunts us with its ambiguity, its existential enormity, its lyrically serpentine language. It's no wonder so many avoid it. Yet poetry uncovers with its alchemy.

Well-crafted poetry requires us to notice, to listen. A poem unfolding, line by line, is a discovery. Unlike utilitarian writing, poetry creates that indescribable anticipation mentioned in Wassiliwizky's study: "[Poetry] valorizes the unconscious, opening us up to new perspectives. [. . .] When every aspect of a poem comes together—form, cadence, emotional appeal—it doesn't just provide the literal chills that Wassiliwizky examined. [. . .] it instills a feeling of a great unknown" (Delistraty). It unsettles us, wakes us from our daily tedium. Williams's poem "The Red Wheelbarrow" suggests the significance of a single tool for the sustenance of family, a farm, and beyond, meditating on an object in slender, specific, ordinary language. The poem annoys many who feel there is no artistry without linguistic or symbolic obfuscation; others distrust such deceptive simplicity. The poem must mean more than this glimpse of a common thing that we would likely overlook. Poems make big things small and microcosms immense.

We come to the communal text of poetry innately tied to some preternatural understanding that, even when words are never exactly enough, they are almost all we have. Ultimately, poetry "is first and last the document of a human experience" (Zavatsky). As poet Ocean Vuong remarked during a reading on our campus, through poetry we can reclaim our stories, our histories; the "language leads back to a life." Great works of art can inspire us to be our best selves; they will sit with us in sadness and joy, meditating on mortality and humanity. Regardless of milieu, poetry confirms we are not alone in the expansive dark.

## WORKS CITED

"About William Carlos Williams." poetryarchive.org/poet/william-carlos-williams

Collins, Billy. "Introduction to Poetry." *Poetry Foundation*, Poetry Foundation. poetryfoundation.org/poems/46712/introduction-to-poetry.

Delistraty, Cody. "This Is What Happens to Your Brain When You Read Poetry." *The Cut.* 11 May 2017. thecut.com/2017/05/this-is-what-happens-to-your-brain-when-you-read-poetry.html

MacLeish, Archibald. "Ars Poetica." *Poetry Foundation*, Poetry Foundation. poetryfoundation.org/poetrymagazine/poems/17168/ars-poetica

Mills, Billy. "Finding the Right Words to Define Poetry." *The Guardian*, 25 Jan. 2008, theguardian.com/books/booksblog/2008/jan/25/findingtherightwordstodef

Pound, Ezra. "A Retrospect" and "A Few Don't's." *Poetry Foundation*, Poetry Foundation, poetryfoundation.org/articles/69409/a-retrospect-and-a-few-donts

"In a Station of the Metro." *Poetry Foundation*, Poetry Foundation, poetryfoundation.org/poetrymagazine/poems/12675/in-a-station-of-the-metr

Ames, Lois and Linda Gray Sexton, eds. *Anne Sexton: A Self-Portrait in Letters.* Boston: Houghton Mifflin, 1977.

Shelly, Percy Bysshe. "A Defence of Poetry." *Poetry Foundation*, Poetry Foundation. poetryfoundation.org/articles/69388/a-defence-of-poetry

Spengemann, William C. and Jessica F. Roberts, eds. Introduction. *Nineteenth Century American Poetry.* 1965. Penguin Classics, 1996.

Williams, William Carlos. "The Red Wheelbarrow." *Poetry Foundation*, Poetry Foundation. poetryfoundation.org/poems/45502/the-red-wheelbarrow

Zavatsky, Bill. "Everything You Ever Wanted to Know about Poetry." *Academy of American Poets*, Academy of American Poets. poets.org/poetsorg/text/everything-you-always-wanted-know-about-poetry

## UNDERSTANDING POETRY WRITING PROMPTS

1. Consider the function of poetry as an art, one of music, meditation, distillation of a moment or slowing time, storytelling, political or social critique, historical record, or as communal text. Why is this function significant to our larger need to connect, right injustices, and understand ourselves, one another, our world/the-natural world/our space in the universe?

2. There is no one agreed-upon definition for what poetry is, yet, how do we define it, traditionally? Is this definition fully accurate based on what we have explored and heard from our presenters? Ultimately, what should ideal poetry be or do? Where does your definition reside within this larger, ongoing conversation?

3. Consider the possibilities that poetry can explore, from the effect of both lyric and/or narrative poems, or the power of brief, epigrammatic forms, object or thing poems, persona poems, nature and eco poems, explorations of family and self, coming of age and identity, the ballad tradition/songs. In relation to one of these categories, consider poetic structure, traditional form poetry versus free verse.

How does structure enhance and further meaning; what might the form mean in relation to the emotion/tone/content of the poem?

4. How do you respond to a poet's poetry on the page versus hearing the poems aloud? What transforms in these various modes of delivery? Poetry is an auditory art that emphasizes musicality; consider the relationship between a physically present audience and the performer, and the ways poems transform from page to stage.

JOANN DEIUDICIBUS

# FIRST SNOW

White hush muffles
birdsong and car-whir.

Storm silence slows
slim veins of water, stills

branch-sway, weekend rush.
Banks rise: bodies breathing.

The glint of everything unsaid
in the slippery dark.

published in *Shawangunk Review*,
volume XXVI, Spring 2015

JOANN DEIUDICIBUS

# SURVIVOR'S GUILT

*Prepare yourself.*
Prepare your shoeless feet for
paths scattered with stone, shells, bone-shatter, casings.

There will be flowers,
stems bound like limbs,
bunches of legs dangling above water;
flowers pulled from fields,
dug from torn ground, rootless.

There will be blood-black blooms,
mud-colored hair spilling like petals,
dark shards arranged in sharp angles.

Those chosen could not prepare:
Captives cast off like chaff
or thrown atop pyres,
stalks askew, barbed leaves lifting
like ash-flecked palms in prayer.

*Prepare yourself.*
The rampart about your heart bursting with grief,
as shrapnel seeps into tight red bud.

published in *Shawangunk Review*,
volume XXI, Spring 2010

# THE POEM IN THE MIRROR

WHEN I TEACH THE ART AND CRAFT OF POETRY as well as when I read and write it, I keep three components in mind. These three words have served me and most of my students well in both creating and discussing poems. They are: theme, image and language. In a class or workshop situation, I try not to use these concepts to over-analyze a poem, but to offer them as guides to open up the poem to its range of creative energy that the poet (as reader and writer) will want to examine.

## THEME:

Basic questions can be asked of all poems: What is the poem about? Is there a central idea that is explored? Do additional ideas rise to the surface, and what thoughts do these stimulate? How is the poet conveying all this to their reader?

As a poet, you can be an open door or a closed door about your interior thoughts. You can make your work easily accessible to your reader, or you can create something more mysterious. However, I feel that a poet should not be so oblique, so dense in their ideas, that they are not letting their reader/listener into the poem. The poet is a writing artist, and writing poetry is not an academic endeavor, although when writing in a fixed form (the sonnet, sestina, haiku, etc.) there are guidelines in which the poet needs to work. But whatever the form, there needs to be a door or entryway that can open and will lead the reader/listener to their own personal meaning and enjoyment of the poem.

## IMAGERY:

Poems can be puzzles. Kaleidoscopes. Word pictures (to bring back an elementary school idea). They allow us to see the world in different ways and through different eyes. Things stand for other things. Words might have layered meanings. A writer once told me—if you want to write about love, write about garbage cans. A funny quip, but I got the message. Conceal (or wrap up) the truth you want to address in a sensory or descriptive image. Invite your reader to find the truth beneath the surface. Be aware, of course, that you should give your reader access to the truth that you are exploring. No reader wants to be frustrated by images in poetic lines that can't be decoded, deciphered, or given access to. Again, there is a thin line between the mysterious and the obscure. Perhaps the poet shouldn't write in an interior, secret code that only they can decipher. A poem is the attempt to reach out to a reader in a condensed, distilled piece of writing. It remains, arguably, the most powerful form of communal writing that we, as humans, have created. And I feel that a poet's main goal is to communicate.

## LANGUAGE:

Some say that poetry is the last bastion of using and playing with language. Free yourself from day-to-day-chatty-talk (unless, of course, that's the language that the poem requires); a poem is often too distilled for chit-chat. However, a poem can utilize clear, simple words to convey its themes and images.

One doesn't have to sound "poetic" to make a poem work, but the writer has to be constantly aware of word choice (vocabulary), word and phrase sequence, and how much to say in a limited framework. You can play with words that are outside of your standard vocabulary. Do you ever use a thesaurus to find a unique word or what may indeed be the "right" word? Feel free to make up words that have never been uttered. Those might indeed be the "right words."

>

> Writers of poetry will nearly almost overwrite a poem. But first drafts should include . . . everything. Once you have your ideas and images on the page or screen, then the real work begins. Crafting, rewriting, reworking. But don't make this drudgery. It should be the opposite—the joy of working on the poem until you reach that draft that comes as close to the truth as you are able (until tomorrow, when you begin to rework it to get even closer).

There is a cosmic joke about writing a poem. It goes like this: 1. Write the poem. 2. Delete the last line. Amusing, perhaps, but there is some truth to this. Often we'll write the poem, then at the end, some literary demon will sit on our shoulder and we'll add a last line that explains the poem to the reader. Try to steer clear of this. Your reader wants to discover your poem, not be told what it means.

Last, a brief word on line length and stanzas: Even in free verse, be aware of where you want to break a line and if you want to create stanzas that become units of language that hold a single thought. Be aware not only of what you are writing (the content) but how you want to arrange and present these words. Every poem that you write may want to explore how and where its words flow onto the page.

**AN OPENING EXERCISE:**

When I begin a poetry workshop or class, I want to find out from each poet what their relationship to poetry is and how they formed these thoughts. I begin by having them draw a line down the middle of a blank notebook page. On the left side, they write the positive thoughts and feelings they have about poetry. Then on the right side of the page, they write any negative thoughts and feelings they have. I ask them to expand their lists and to include positive and negative thoughts about their first exposure to poetry; how poetry was taught to them; their own work; reading the poems of others; reading and hearing poems at public events; submitting and publishing, etc. The lists become longer than the poets would have imagined. Next, we share the lists, first in small groups, then as a full group. These discussions create both humorous and deep responses and directly lead to a poetry prompt.

The group is asked to write a metapoem: a poem about poetry or your relationship with poetry. This poem should be between 8 and 20 lines long. Poets can structure it on the page however they like. After a writing session, we share first drafts in small groups. The poets are then free to work on these first drafts on their own and bring in newer drafts to share with the group. This exercise has been a good one to begin sharing additional poems and to discuss them in future sessions.

# THE POET'S WALK

You may have heard these words from someone.
Or perhaps you heard them in a dream.

A poem leads you down a path to a clearing
where light can filter through. To a place where
the truth and the past sit silently with legs crossed.

You can hear them speaking faintly, something about you.
They never catch your eye or offer you an answer,
but they might pass on a word or phrase that somehow

you have missed. And when they tell you what they can,
they'll send you on your way. Back to the place you live
your life. And once you're there, you'll remember something

that you never knew. The mirror gazing back. The dark
without dread. The face of the one you long to see.
And only you will recognize these offerings.

But they're yours now.
To keep or give away.

# WRITING

1.
pencil skates on sheets
wood on wood like skin on skin
a lover's intrigue

2.
pen chases paper
words that sketch the reader's eye
shadows in the cave

3.
fingers click keyboard
past present future perfect
all roads lead this way

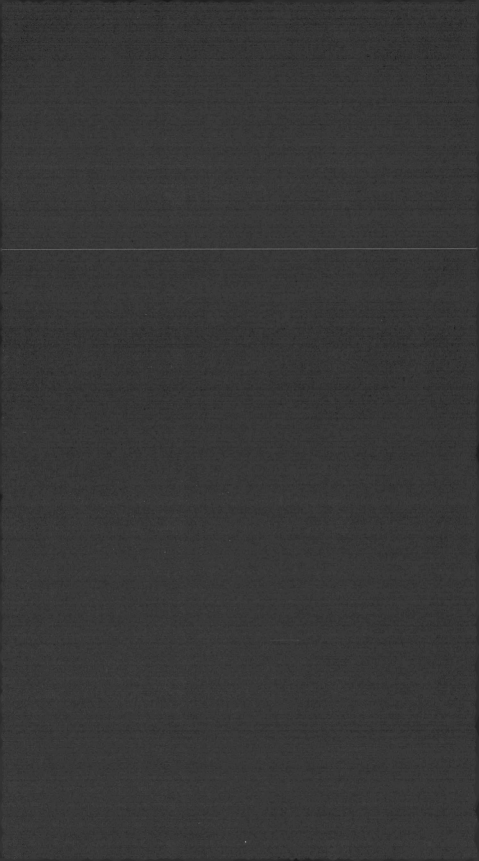

# AIRWORDS: DOING JUSTICE TO YOUR SPOKEN POEMS IN YOUR READINGS

## BY LAURENCE CARR AND CLAIRE HERO

My colleague and fellow poet Claire Hero and I are often saddened by how unfocused many poets are when they read their own work aloud in public readings, be they in informal workshops or in more formal venues at literary events and book launch presentations. Many poets don't understand that in reading their work in public, there is a performance aspect to that experience. I'm not saying that a poet must perform as an actor would (and reading one's work is not a stand-up routine or one's "party-piece"), but poets often don't help their own cause. When one reads in public, there is triangle of connection through which creative electricity must flow. The poet must connect with their text, with their audience, and also with themselves if they are going to have the "people out front" not only listen to the text, but hear it on a deeper level. Claire and I put together some guidelines to help poets (especially poets who haven't read in public enough to feel comfortable) through the danger/anxiety zone of reading their words to a group. These ideas may seem elementary (and they are), but in the heat of the moment, we often forget the basics.

— Laurence Carr, editor

## SOME RECOMMENDED GUIDELINES:

### POSITIVES:

1. Rehearse your work prior to the event.

2. Visually take in the space in which you are going to read.

3. Take a moment to prepare yourself physically and mentally.

4. It's OK to be nervous; that means you want to do a good reading.

5. Your audience has come to enjoy your work; you should, too.

6. Read the last line of your work with the same energy as you read the first lines (from Speech Class 101: Don't drop your voice unless you're creating an effect).

7. The meaning of a line can be conveyed through emphasis, pauses and voice modulations. This doesn't mean you have to "act." Simply—don't be boring.

8. Remember to breathe.

9. Bring closure to the piece so your audience knows that it has ended.

10. Accept the energy that your audience gives you and respect that.

11. Enjoy this moment of giving your creative work.

**NEGATIVES:**

1. Don't be late and rush into the room or up to the reader's area.

2. Don't apologize for your work.

3. Don't tell the audience that you "Just wrote this." (You can say that this is a new piece.)

4. Don't try to read from illegible copies.

5. Don't read from memory if you haven't memorized the piece.

6. Don't speak too softly or too fast; Project your words so everyone can hear.

7. Don't abuse the audience's attention span; Respect the time limits that have been established for the reading. If you are asked to read one poem, read one poem, not four.

8. Don't appear visibly relieved to have come to the end of your reading.

9. Don't get flustered or comment if you lose your place; just find it and go on.

10. Either at the beginning or the end, don't explain what the poem is about unless you are part of a Q&A afterwards. And even then be brief; it's not an analysis class.

11. Your introduction to a poem should not be longer than the poem.

12. Learn how to use a mic. And practice.

# CONTRIBUTORS

DAVID APPELBAUM treads a thin line between poetry and philosophy. A professor of philosophy at SUNY New Paltz, his work, in a series of books, focuses on the transcendent nature of ordinary things, including *Everyday Spirits* [SUNY Press, 1995]. In addition, his thought shows a special interest in the performance of the speaking voice. For ten years, he was editor-in-chief of *Parabola Magazine*, with its concern for wisdom traditions and the search for meaning. As Publisher of Codhill Press, an independent literary small press which he founded fifteen years ago, he has produced a booklist of nearly one hundred titles, including authors of international reputation. A number of collections of his own poems have been published, including most recently *Jiggerweed* [Finishing Line Press, 2011], *Vespers* [Hammer and Anvil Books, 2012], *Letters and Found Poems of Edisa and Chloe* [Codhill Press, 2013], and *notes on water: an aqueous phenomenology* [Monkfish, 2017].

CELIA BLAND's third collection of poetry, *Cherokee Road Kill*, will be published in 2017. The title poem was awarded the 2015 Raynes Prize, judged by L.S. Asekoff. Selected prints of the *Madonna Comix*, a image and poetry collaboration created with artist Dianne Kornberg, were exhibited at New York City's Lesley Heller Gallery, at Bard College at Simon's Rock as part of the Berkshire Women Writers Festival. The book *Madonna Comix* was reviewed in the spring issue of *Drunken Boat*. Her work has recently appeared in *Storyscape*, *Drunken Boat*, *Gulf Coast*, and the *Cortland Review*, among others.

SALLY BLIUMIS-DUNN teaches modern poetry and Creative Writing at Manhattanville College. She received her B.A. in Russian language and literature from U.C. Berkeley in 1983 and her MFA from Sarah Lawrence College in 2002. In 2002, she was a finalist for the Nimrod/Hardman Pablo Neruda prize. Her poems have been published in *The Paris Review*, *Prairie Schooner*, *Poetry London* and *The New York Times*, among others. In 2008, she was asked to read in the Love Poems program at the Library of Congress. She lives in Armonk, New York. Her first book, *Talking Underwater*, was published in 2007 by Wind Publications. Her second book, *Second Skin*, was published by Wind Publications in 2010.

>

> CORY BROWN'S latest collection of poems was published in 2014 by *Cayuga Lake Books*. His poems have appeared in *Bomb, Nimrod International*, and *Postmodern Culture*, among others. He also publishes personal essays, which have appeared in *South Loop Review, Journal of Narrative Politics*, and (forthcoming) *Writing on the Edge*. He teaches poetry and essay writing at Ithaca College, as well as courses in intellectual history, such as the history of the pursuit of happiness, the history of Western concepts of self since the Renaissance, and the philosophy and science of sex and love.

LAURENCE CARR (editor) writes poetry, fiction, and plays. Two poetry collections, *Threnodies: poems in remembrance* and *The Wytheport Tales* are published by Codhill Press with whom he also edited *WaterWrites: A Hudson River Anthology* (co-editor); *Riverine: An Anthology of Hudson Valley Writers* and *A Slant of Light: Contemporary Women Writers of the Hudson Valley* (co-edited with Jan Zlotnik Schmidt) which won the 2013 USA Best Book Award for Fiction Anthology. His play, *Kennedy at Colonus* was cited in the *Burns Mantle Best Plays Series* and is published as an eBook. His writing has been widely published and over 20 of his plays have been produced throughout the U.S and Europe. His novel, *Pancake Hollow Primer*, won the Next Generation Indie Book Award for first novel in 2012. Laurence has taught creative and dramatic writing at SUNY New Paltz for over twenty years. www.carrwriter.com

LUCIA CHERCIU is a Professor of English at SUNY / Dutchess Community College in Poughkeepsie, NY, and writes both in English and in Romanian. Her books include *Train Ride to Bucharest* (Sheep Meadow Press, 2017), *Edible Flowers* (Main Street Rag, 2015), *Lalele din Paradis / Tulips in Paradise* (Eikon, 2017), *Altoiul Râsului / Grafted Laughter* (Brumar 2010), and *Lepădarea de Limbă / The Abandonment of Language* (Vinea, 2009). Her poetry was nominated twice for a Pushcart Prize and Best of the Net. www.luciacherciu.webs.com

SUSAN CHUTE is the founder and presenter of Next Year's Words (www.facebook.com/NPNextYearsWords/), a popular reading series in New Paltz mixing community and academic creative writers, now beginning its fourth year. Her poem "Pulse," about the Orlando tragedy, was published online at *The Brillantina Project* thebrillantinaproject. wordpress.com/2016/07/08/pulse and other poems were published in the *Wallkill Valley Writer's Anthology 2015* (www.amazon.com/Wallkill-

Valley-Writers-Anthology-2015/dp/0986093637) and in various
obscure feminist periodicals. She prefers the immediate gratification of
a live audience for her work, and is quite lackadaisical about submitting
it to print & online journals. Many moons ago, she taught an *Introduction
to Poetry* course at the University of Pittsburgh. As a librarian presiding
over the Art and Picture Collections at The New York Public Library, she
taught another poetry class called *The Colored Line, the Pictured Word*. Now
she digs through archives at Women's Studio Workshop and gives tours
of Lincoln Center. And writes poems.

SUZANNE CLEARY won the John Ciardi Prize for Poetry for her third
book, *Beauty Mark*, published in 2013 by BkMk Press of the University
of Missouri-Kansas City. Her other awards include a Pushcart Prize,
the Cecil Hemley Memorial Award of the Poetry Society of America, a
fellowship from the New York Foundation for the Arts, and residencies
at Yaddo and the MacDowell Colony. Her publication credits include the
journals *Poetry London, Georgia Review, Southern Review,* and *New Ohio
Review,* and the anthologies *Best American Poetry* and *Poetry 180*. She holds
an M.A. in Writing from Washington University and a Ph.D. in Literature
and Criticism from Indiana University of Pennsylvania. Professor of
English at the State University of New York at Rockland, Cleary also
teaches as core faculty in the Converse College low-residency MFA
Program in Creative Writing. Her website is
www.suzanneclearypoet.com. BkMk Press will publish a volume in 2018.

JOANN K. DEIUDICIBUS is the Staff Assistant for the Composition
Program and an Adjunct Instructor at SUNY New Paltz, where she earned
her MA in English (2003). She is the Associate Editor (poetry) for
*WaterWrites: A Hudson River Anthology* (Codhill Press, 2009). Her poems
have been published in *A Slant of Light: Contemporary Women Writers of the
Hudson Valley* (Codhill Press, 2013), *Chronogram,* and around the Hudson
Valley. Her article, "Axing the Frozen Sea: Female Inscriptions of
Madness" was included in the anthology *Affective Disorder and the Writing
Life: The Melancholic Muse* (Palgrave Macmillan, 2014). Her research
interests include creativity, mental health, and composition, the body,
as well as twentieth-century American poetry, particularly the work of
Anne Sexton.

>

DENNIS DOHERTY teaches creative writing and literature at SUNY New Paltz. He is author of four volumes of poetry – *The Bad Man* (Ye Olde Font Shoppe Press, 2004), *Fugitive* (Codhill Press, 2007), *Crush Test* (Codhill Press, 2010), and *Black Irish* (Codhill Press, 2016), as well as an extended meditation on Twain's great novel: *Why Read The Adventures of Huckleberry Finn* (New Street Communication, 2014). His essays, poems, and stories appear throughout the literary press.

ANNE GORRICK is a poet and visual artist. She is the author of six books of poetry including: *An Absence So Great and Spontaneous it is Evidence of Light* (forthcoming from the Operating System, 2018); and *The Olfactions: Poems on Perfume* (BlazeVOX Books, 2017). She co-edited (with poet Sam Truitt) *In|Filtration: An Anthology of Innovative Writing from the Hudson River Valley* (Station Hill Press, 2016). From 2006-2014, she curated 50 readings in series Cadmium Text. With Melanie Klein, she curates the reading series *Process to Text*, which focuses on innovative writing from in and around New York's Hudson Valley. She is President of the Board of Trustees at Century House Historical Society, home of the Widow Jane Mine, an all-volunteer organization (www.centuryhouse.org) that hosts a variety of arts events, and preserves the history of the now-defunct local cement industry. Anne Gorrick lives in West Park, New York.

LEA GRAHAM is the author of the forthcoming book, *From the Hotel Vernon* (Salmon Press, 2019), the chapbook, *This End of the World: Notes to Robert Kroetsch* (Apt. 9 Press, 2016) and the poetry book, *Hough & Helix & Where & Here & You, You, You* (No Tell Books, 2011). She is an associate professor at Marist College in Poughkeepsie, NY and a native of Northwest Arkansas.

CAROL GRASER hosts the monthly poetry series at Saratoga Spring's legendary Caffè Lena on the first Wednesday of every month and has performed her work at various events and venues around NYS. Her work has been published in many literary journals, recently in *Devilfish Review*, *Punch Drunk Press*, *Trailer Park Quarterly* and *Minute Magazine*. She is the author of the poetry collection, *The Wild Twist of Their Stems*.

CLAIRE HERO is the author of the full-length collection *Sing, Mongrel* and three chapbooks: *afterpastures*, winner of the 2008 Caketrain Chapbook competition, *Cabinet*, and *Dollyland*. Her poems have appeared in such journals as *Bennington Review*, *Black Warrior Review*, *Cincinnati Review*, *Copper Nickel*, and *Denver Quarterly*, and have also been included in the anthologies *IN/FILTRATION*, *A Slant of Light: Contemporary Women Writers of the Hudson Valley*, and *narrative(dis)continuities: prose experiments by younger american writers*. She moved to the Hudson Valley in 2008 and now teaches at SUNY New Paltz and Marist College.

KATHARYN HOWD MACHAN, author of 37 collections of poetry (most recently, in 2018, her *Selected Poems* from FutureCycle Press and *Secret Music: Voices from Redwing, 1888* from Cayuga Lake Books) has lived in Ithaca, New York, since 1975 and, now as a full professor, has taught Writing at Ithaca College since 1977. After many years of coordinating the Ithaca Community Poets and directing the Feminist Women's Writing Workshops, Inc., she was selected to be Tompkins County's first poet laureate. Her poems have appeared in numerous magazines, anthologies, and textbooks, and she has edited three thematic anthologies.

KATE HYMES is a poet and writer, writing consultant, workshop leader and editor. Her poetry has been published in *Gathering Ground: Cave Canem 10 Year Anniversary Anthology*, University of Michigan Press, *Riverine: An Anthology of Hudson Valley Writers*, and *A Slant of Light: Contemporary Women Writers of the Hudson Valley*. She edited wVw Anthologies 2011 and 2015, is an online editor for wallkillvalleywriters. org, and has led writing workshops in the Hudson Valley for 25 years. She serves on the board of *Amherst Writers and Artists*, an international arts organization, and *Calling All Poets*, New Paltz, NY.

MIKE JURKOVIC is a 2016 Pushcart nominee; his poetry and musical criticism have appeared in innumerable magazines and periodicals with little reportable income. Full-length collections: *smitten by harpies & shiny banjo catfish* (Lion Autumn Press, 2016) Chapbooks, *Eve's Venom* (Post Traumatic Press, 2014) *Purgatory Road* (Pudding House, 2010) *blue fan whirring*, a collection of haiku & short poems, due 2017, Nirala Press. Anthologies: *WaterWrites* and *Riverine* (Codhill Press, 2009, 2007). President, Calling All Poets Series, New Paltz and Beacon, NY. Producer of CAPSCASTS, performances from Calling All Poets Series. Features & CD reviews appear in *All About Jazz* and the *Van Wyck Gazette*. He loves Emily most of all. www.mikejurkovic.com  www.callingallpoets.net

RAPHAEL KOSEK's poems have appeared in such venues as *Poetry East*, *Catamaran*, and *Briar Cliff Review*. Her latest chapbook, *Rough Grace* won the 2014 Concrete Wolf Chapbook Prize. Her lyric essays won first prize at *Bacopa Review* (2017) and *Eastern Iowa Review* (2016). Her full-length poetry manuscript, *American Mythology*, was a 2017 finalist at Grayson Books. She teaches English at Marist College and Dutchess Community College.

>

MOLLY McGLENNEN was born and raised in Minneapolis, Minnesota and is of Anishinaabe and European descent. Currently, she is an Associate Professor of English and Native American Studies at Vassar College. She earned a PhD in Native American Studies from University of California, Davis and an MFA in Creative Writing from Mills College. Her creative writing and scholarship have been published widely. She is the author of a collection of poetry *Fried Fish and Flour Biscuits*, published by Salt's award-winning "Earthworks Series" of Indigenous writers, and a critical monograph *Creative Alliances: The Transnational Designs of Indigenous Women's Poetry* from University of Oklahoma Press, which earned the Beatrice Medicine Award for outstanding scholarship in American Indian Literature. Currently, she is working on a second book of poems about Indigenous Minneapolis.

TED MILLAR teaches English at Mahopac High School, and creative writing and poetry at Marist College. His poems have appeared in *Caesura, Circle Show, The Broke Bohemian The Voices Project, Third Wednesday, Tiny Poetry: Macropoetrics, Scintilla, GFT Press, Inklette, The Grief Diaries, Cactus Heart, Aji, Wordpool Press, The Artistic Muse, Chronogram, Brickplight*, and *Inkwell*. In addition to writing poetry, he is also a frequent contributor to *Liberal America* and *Liberal Liberal Nation Rising*. He lives in the heart of apple and wine country in New York's Hudson Valley with his wife and two children.

JUDITH SAUNDERS is Professor of English at Marist College, where she has taught writing courses of many kinds, including workshops in poetic form, prose and verse parody, satire and humor, and personal essays and memoir. A specialist in contemporary English and American poetry, she has published commentary on Elizabeth Bishop, Charles Tomlinson, Gwendolyn Brooks, Howard Moss, May Swenson, Kay Ryan, Billy Collins, and others. Her own poems have appeared in a wide variety of periodicals and anthologies, and she is the author of two prize-winning chapbooks. Her most recent work can be found in *Blue Unicorn, Chiron Review, Snowy Egret*, and *Isle*.

JAN ZLOTNIK SCHMIDT is a SUNY Distinguished Teaching Professor of English at SUNY New Paltz. She has been published in many journals including *The Cream City Review, Kansas Quarterly, The Alaska Quarterly Review, Home Planet News, Phoebe, Black Buzzard Review, The Chiron Review, Memoir(and), The Westchester Review*, and *Wind*. Her work has been nominated for the Pushcart Press Prize Series. She has had two volumes of poetry published by the Edwin Mellen Press (*We Speak in Tongues*, 1991; *She had this memory*, 2000). Her chapbook, *The Earth Was Still*, was published by Finishing Line Press and another, *Hieroglyphs of Father-Daughter Time*, was published by Word Temple Press. Most recently she co-edited with Laurence Carr a collection of works by Hudson Valley women writers entitled *A Slant of Light: Contemporary Women Writers of the Hudson Valley*.

MARGO TAFT STEVER's four poetry collections are *The Lunatic Ball*, Kattywompus Press, 2015; *The Hudson Line*, Main Street Rag, 2012; *Frozen Spring*, Mid-List Press First Series Award for Poetry, 2002; and *Reading the Night Sky*, Riverstone Poetry Chapbook Competition, 1996. In 2019, *CRACKED PIANO*, will be published by CavanKerry Press. Her poems have appeared widely in literary magazines including *Blackbird, Salamander, Prairie Schooner*, The Academy of American Poet's *Poem-A-Day, New England Review, Cincinnati Review, Rattapallax, Webster Review*, and anthologies including *Dire Elegies, Chance of a Ghost*, and *No More Masks*. She is the founder of The Hudson Valley Writers' Center and the founding and current co-editor of Slapering Hol Press. For more information, please see: www.margostever.com

PAULINE UCHMANOWICZ is an Associate Professor of English and Director of the Creative Writing Program at SUNY New Paltz and is the author of poetry collections *Starfish* (2016), *Inchworm Season* (2010), and *Sand & Traffic* (2004). Her poems, essays, and reviews have appeared widely, including in *Commonweal, Crazyhorse, Massachusetts Review, New American Writing, Ohio Review, Ploughshares, Radcliffe Quarterly, Southern Poetry Review*, and *Z Magazine*. She is cofounder and series editor of the Codhill Poetry Award, established in 2004.

ROBERT WAUGH is now a professor emeritus of the English Department at SUNY New Paltz, where he still teaches an occasional course. He has published poems in several literary journals, as well as publishing two books of poems in Codhill Press, *Shoreward, Tideward* and *Thumbtacks, Glass, Pennies*. In addition he has published two critical books on the works of H. P. Lovecraft in Hippocampus Press, *The Monster in the Mirror* and *A Monster of Voices*; in that press a collection of his weird tales has recently appeared in 2015, with the title *The Bloody Tugboat and Other Witcheries*. He is now writing other critical essays, stories and poems.